MW00899759

THE RADICAL SELF-LOVE WORKBOOK FOR ADULTS

A MINDFULNESS GUIDE WITH DAILY CBT EXERCISES
TO BREAK FREE FROM SELF-CRITICISM, DOUBT AND
SOCIAL ANXIETY (BOOST CONFIDENCE, SELF-
ESTEEM, HAPPINESS)

S. S. LEIGH

Special Bonus!

Want This Bonus Book for FREE?

Get <u>FREE</u>, unlimited access to it and all my new books by joining the Fan Base!

SCAN W/ YOUR CAMERA TO JOIN!

"You yourself, as much as anybody in the entire universe, deserve your love and affection." —Buddha

CONTENTS

INTRODUCTION

Around 10 years ago, I had a serious problem – I wanted others to love me, but I didn't love myself! I was frustrated, desperate, and depressed. I could not understand why I was so unfortunate that every relationship I got into would fall apart. It wasn't hard to tell that all my romantic relationships followed the same pattern. They would start on a high note, and then, as soon as I would become genuinely invested in the relationship, the other person would pull away.

I would desperately try holding onto that person, but in my heart, I always knew – it was over! For years, I cried myself to sleep every night. I felt overwhelmed by these questions – "Why me?" "Why am I the only person in the world who can't stay in a relationship?" "Am I ever going to get married?" "Why does love elude me every single time?"

I was so deeply trapped inside my victim mindset that I couldn't recognize the role I was playing in the destruction of my relationships. Besides, it wasn't just my romantic relationships that were dysfunctional. Pretty much all my relationships were in shambles.

I felt lonely and dejected every single day. Simply staying alive felt like the hardest thing I had to do every single day. There were so many days when merely getting out of bed seemed like a massive accomplishment. I dreaded mornings because very morning when the sun would come up, I'd realize that the option of escaping into dreamland was no longer available to me. I had to face reality – the reality that I was lonely and miserable. Nothing in my life was going the way I would like it to.

I felt like a loser – a total failure. It had become impossible for me to hold on to a job or to a relationship. Even my family didn't want to be around me. I had no real friends. I often turned to food and television for comfort. My 'reality' was so excruciatingly painful that I was able to find comfort only in the world of make-believe.

One day I had a major altercation with my boss at work. It made me really upset. I felt certain that I was going to lose my job. To escape the pain and misery I was feeling, I headed to a bar right after the workday ended. Over there, I got so drunk that to this day I have no clear recollection of exactly what happened on that evening. All I can remember is I got in my car to go back home and then a giant tree showed up out of nowhere. I felt terrified that the tree was going to devour me. After that, I blacked out completely.

When I came back to my senses, I was in a hospital bed with all kinds of tubes and pipes attached to my body. At first, I had no idea where I was or how I got there in the first place. Very soon I learned that I had experienced a head-on colli-sion with a giant tree while driving back home. My car had been completely damaged in the accident. It was a miracle that I was still alive!

The next few days were very hard. Every inch of my body was hurting. I wasn't able to eat food or drink water prop-erly. It was in those darkest hours of my life that I had a profound realization. I didn't want to die – I wanted to live. It's just that I wanted a better life than what I had had until that point.

At that moment, I also realized that I had been taking so much for granted. When it was excruciatingly painful to swallow food or drink water, I suddenly realized that even the ability to swallow food and drink water is a huge blessing. It is so tragic that we don't understand the value of what we have until it is taken away from us. In those moments, I learned that nothing in life should ever be taken for granted.

That day I made a promise to myself – I was going to improve my life! I committed to doing whatever it takes to turn my dream life into a reality. I decided that I was either going to succeed in creating my dream life or I'd die trying. Even the latter felt like a far better proposition than the idea of continuing to waste my life writhing in self-pity and indulging in self-destructive behavior. I wanted to be genuinely happy, and, this time, I had decided I wasn't going to sit around waiting for happiness to come find me. I was going to proactively do whatever it takes to become the happiest, most joyful person I can ever be.

Once I got out of the hospital, my passionate quest for self-improvement began. I signed up for a gym membership so I could take excellent care of my body. Next, I added a simple five-minute meditation to my morning routine. I became steadfastly committed to my newly adopted self-care regime.

From that point on, self-improvement became my obsession and passion. I studied any valuable information I could find on the subject - be it through courses, books, mentors, or coaches. At that stage of my life, I was so desperate to feel better that I was willing to **try anything** and everything that could possibly help me on any **level**.

Slowly, things started improving. I began feeling better about myself. Most importantly, I began to understand who I was, what I wanted, and **who** I wanted to be in this life. Eventually, I was also able to **find** another job that was better aligned with my core values **and** talents.

I still had days when I would struggle to get out of bed. Sometimes, I would even **slip back** into full-blown depression and dejection. But I **was** also learning to be more resilient. I realized that it **didn't** matter how many times I fell down. What matters is how **quickly** I can get back up on my feet again.

FALL IN LOVE WITH *yourself*

As I made progress on my self-improvement journey, the amount of time I needed to **get** myself back up kept reducing. Even now, there are **days when** I fall down but I have trained myself to get back **up** immediately. If you'll follow everything that I will be **teaching** you in this book, then you'll be able to do the same as well.

Going back to my story, I started spending a lot of time at a local bookstore that specializes in self-help and spirituality-related books. I would spend hours in the bookshop browsing through self-improvement books. One day a book caught my eye. I felt powerfully drawn towards it. It was a book on CBT (Cognitive Behavioral Techniques). I flipped through the first few pages and I immediately knew I had to buy it.

This is how I got introduced to the world of CBT. Since then, I have read countless books on this subject. My problem with most CBT books is that they are often too academic and full of hard-to-understand jargons. As a reader, I would have liked a book that was simple and easy to understand. I wanted practical guidance on how to immediately start applying everything I was learning to my own life.

I am writing this book now for you because this is the book I wish I had when I was looking for guidance. I had to learn things the hard way through a lot of trial and error. With this book, I want to simplify the process for you so that you can apply CBT to your life a lot more easily and, thereby, get results much faster.

Quite early on in my self-improvement journey, I realized that my relationships with others were never going to work unless I improved the most important relationship in my life – my relationship with myself! By using CBT techniques and methods, I was able to take practical action to change my life, my emotions, and my mind.

I hope this book will guide you to love yourself. I am sharing my best techniques, tools, and methods with you here. I will only ever share with you what has worked for me personally. I hope this book will help you create a happier and more fulfilling life for yourself.

No matter what you are going through right now, you have the power and the ability to emerge victorious. I believe in you!

DECLARATION OF COMMITMENT

The extent to which you are going to benefit from this book depends entirely upon the level of commitment you have towards absorbing all the information I am sharing here and doing all the exercises. To get results, you have to go all in. If you are ready, then write your name and sign the statement of declaration. If you feel you aren't ready yet, then come back again after some time once you feel you are ready to go all in.

I would highly recommend that you use this book every single day until you have studied all the information and completed all the exercises. Even if all you can manage is a few paragraphs a day, it is better than sporadically using the workbook. Consistency is the master key to success. You can go at your own pace – just make sure that you are studying each chapter thoroughly and completing all exercises as best as you can.

Write your declaration of commitment here and seal it with your signature.

THIS IS MY BINDING COMMITMENT TO:

_____

_____

_____

_____

_____

Signature

1

DO YOU LOVE YOURSELF?

"Owning our story and loving ourselves through that process is the bravest thing that we'll ever do."

— BRENÉ BROWN

As human beings, we are wired to seek love. The problem is that we are taught from a young age to seek it outside of ourselves instead of focusing on cultivating it within ourselves. No matter how much someone loves you or cares for you, they can never give you what you don't have for yourself. I had to learn this truth the hard way. I desperately kept trying to get others to love me. The irony was the harder I tried, the faster my relationships fell apart.

The problem with expecting someone to give you what you are not giving to yourself is that they could be doing the best that they are capable of, but it may not exactly be what you want. We all desire love, but how each one of us defines and experiences love is often unique to us. We have different needs, and our unique personality traits determine the distinctive way in which we like to give and receive love.

By default, we try to give others what we ourselves want to receive. Hence, the way we give and express love to another person is determined by how we like to receive love ourselves. This is why someone may be doing the very best that they are capable of but it may not feel fulfilling to us. This is simply because they are expressing their love in a language we do not resonate with.

Also, even if you are with someone who gives and receives love in the same way as you do, it doesn't guarantee that you'll feel fulfilled by it. Let me explain this with the help of an analogy. I was sitting by the river bank one day. For fun, I dug up a small hole in the sand and started filling it with water that I brought from the river. As soon as I poured water into the hole I had dug, the water would disappear. At first, I was puzzled. Eventually, I realized the receptacle that I had created in the sand was simply not capable of containing the water inside it.

In the same way, we cannot fully receive and accept someone else's love unless we make ourselves a perfect receptacle for receiving it. Someone can pour all their love and affection onto you, but it may leave you feeling empty and depleted simply because you have not developed the capacity to absorb what they are giving you. You must first build a perfect receptacle by practicing radical self-love.

Self-love is the beginning of every kind of love. I am sure you have already heard the saying that no one can pour from an empty cup. Indeed, you cannot give to someone else what you don't have for yourself. I don't think it is an exaggeration to say that we can truly love another human being without being in love with ourselves first. Trying to pour from an empty cup causes a buildup of resentment and grudges.

It is an unfortunate truth that women are taught to be extremely self-sacrificing from a very young age. Little girls are often conditioned to believe that their needs don't matter. They are taught to put their own needs behind everyone else's. I am not saying that we shouldn't make sacrifices for the greater good of the family unit or for society at large, but if you'll keep doing it all the time, then that is certainly going to deplete you.

I meet so many mothers who feel their family takes them for granted. These wonderful women wake up every morning at the crack of dawn and spend all day catering to the needs of their families. They take no time to look after themselves. By night, they are bone-tired and ready to crash into bed. The problem is that they want to fill everyone else's cup without filling their own first.

Of course, this can be just as true for men as it is for women. In our society, men have their own unique struggles. For instance, they are taught to suppress their emotions and never express their authentic feelings. Men are also expected to make different types of sacrifices for the greater good of family and society. It can lead to resentment and a deep sense of unhappiness if they aren't filling their own cup first.

WHY YOU MUST FILL YOUR OWN CUP FIRST

The biggest problem with not filling your own cup first is that it compels you to have unrealistic expectations of others. You start depending upon other people for your happiness, but there is no one in this world who can fulfill such an expectation (absolutely, no one!). Also, if you don't have unconditional love for yourself, then you just can't have it for another human being either. No matter what you say or believe, it is simply not possible.

The question of someone taking you for granted arises only when you are expecting something in return for what you are giving. Besides, if you are doing things with the expectation of receiving something back, can we really call it unconditional love?

Whenever I am about to do something for someone, I always ask myself one question: "Would I do it even if I received nothing in return – not even an acknowledgment?" If the answer is "yes," then I know it is the right thing for me to do. But if the answer is no, then it would be better for me to not do it.

Saying no is not easy. We want to please others – that isn't necessarily a bad thing. The problem is if you are trying to please someone else by putting yourself in a very uncomfortable position, then you are inevitably going to come out of that experience feeling depleted and resentful. You have to think about yourself first. If you are bargaining your own happiness to please someone else, it's just not worthwhile.

Fill up your own cup first!

You should never do something for someone else expecting something in return. Give to others unconditionally, or don't do it at all. I am not talking about being self-sacrificing here. All I am saying is that you have no control over someone else's behavior no matter how close you are to them. If you are looking for something (even if it is only a desire for acknowledgment or praise), then you are setting yourself up for disappointment.

There is absolutely no guarantee that you are going to receive what you want. If you'll verbally demand that the other person give you what you are looking for, then the chances are even lower that you'll receive it. On the other hand, when you do things for others because that's just what you want, the act itself becomes a reward. If you receive an acknowledgment, praise, or any other reward in return, you're able to appreciate what you are receiving better.

Always remember that you can **never** have a wonderful relationship with another human being without first having a beautiful relationship with yourself. To genuinely love someone else, you have to be in love with yourself first. Hence, self-love is the foremost **kind** of love. If you feel you don't have enough love in your life right now, then it is time you need to start filling your own cup first.

WHAT DOES IT MEAN TO LOVE YOURSELF?

The older I get, the more I realize that love is a verb and not a noun. Unlike what the movies suggest, love doesn't just happen. It has to be cultivated through action and intention. You have to consistently and constantly do things that help you feel loved and cared for.

When couples say they have fallen out of love after having spent a decade or so together, I genuinely feel sorry for them. Pop culture makes people believe that the heady feeling of infatuation is love. This is why people enter relationships expecting it to be all roses and sunshine with no effort required on their part. Would you expect a garden to remain prim and perfect if you never tended to it? How can you expect to have a great relationship with yourself or with others if you aren't intentionally putting in the effort for it.

Relationships make life beautiful, but they also require constant tending to. You have to invest in your relationships if you want them to be amazing and fulfilling. I hope by now, you understand that the most important relationship in your life is the one you have with yourself. You teach others how to treat you by the example of how you are treating yourself.

If you constantly keep bashing yourself and then you wonder why your partner never accepts you for who you are, it is time to look within. Even if you are the only person who is ever going to hear the negative self-talk inside your head, at the energetic level, it impacts every single relationship you are ever going to have. It's not an exaggeration to say that your relationships with others are a reflection of your relationship with yourself.

When I was addicted to finding flaws in my physical appearance, I used to end up with men who were also hyper-critical of my looks. Once I changed my perception of myself and I accepted myself as the amazing person that I am, other people started affirming my awesomeness as well.

Now that we have established that love is a verb defined by action and not just a feeling, let us explore some of the ways in which we can practice self-love. As you read through the next subsections, think about how many of these things you are practicing now. If you aren't already practicing any of these, then think about how you can incorporate these ideas into your life.

At the end of this chapter, I'll also share a quiz with you where you can check your score to see where you stand on the self-love spectrum. It will help you better understand your starting point. When you know what you are starting out with, it becomes easier to know how you need to move forward to achieve your goal.

Talking to and About Yourself with Love

From now on, I want you to become very conscious of your self-talk. What is that voice in your head telling you right now? Does this voice encourage you to achieve your goals or does it keep pulling you down? Does this voice appreciate you or is it constantly criticizing you? Keep in mind the fact that thought is the precursor of all action. How you are talking to yourself determines what kind of action you are taking in your life.

If you are constantly criticizing yourself, then it is likely that you are also not doing much to squash your limiting beliefs. You cannot achieve anything worthwhile in life without first believing that you are worthy and deserving of what you desire.

It is also very important that you start becoming conscious of how you talk about yourself to others. Are you always putting yourself down in front of others or do you talk about yourself with confidence and pride? Now, I am not talking about being cocky. Authentic self-confidence comes from a place of self-love and humility.

When you truly love who you are, you don't feel the need to try and prove yourself to others. You know you are enough and your opinion of yourself is all that truly matters. People who come across as cocky and full of themselves do not really believe in themselves. Their cockiness stems from deep insecurity lying underneath the veneer of over-confidence.

From now on, start becoming more observant and conscious of what you truly think about yourself. The self-talk inside your head and the conversations you are having with others about yourself will give you all the data you need to under-stand how you see yourself.

Another important thing to observe is how you respond to compliments. Do you feel comfortable and uneasy when someone pays a compliment or do you accept compliments graciously? If someone gives you a compliment and you counteract it by putting yourself down, then that means you don't really love yourself. Worse still, it is likely that you don't feel deserving of praise and appreciation.

Feeling Worthy and Deserving

Do you feel worthy and deserving of the good things you already have in your life and of the things you desire? Most of the time we don't get what we want because deep down, we don't feel worthy of it. This can be true for your dream career, your dream marriage, or just about everything else in life.

I used to think there was nothing I wanted more badly than a relationship. For as long back as I can remember, I wanted to get married and have a family of my own. As I shared earlier, I had no issues attracting wonderful potential partners into my life. Things would start off on a high note, but my world would come crashing down equally fast. Yes, I can blame those people and say things like, "There are no good people left in this world." But this isn't the truth.

This world has all kinds of people in it. We don't attract what we want. We attract who we are. When we don't feel worthy and deserving of what we want, we stand in our own way of getting what we want. In my case, I managed to attract the type of potential partner I wanted into my life. Things would start out well and then I would subconsciously start sabotaging the connection.

Deep inside, I felt unworthy of what I was receiving. At the surface level, I thought I was amazing but deep inside I believed I didn't deserve to be loved. I would have a hard time accepting the fact that a wonderful desirable person would want to be with me. My subconscious mind would start looking for signs that the person was cheating on me or worse still, I'll start waiting for them to call things off with me. Eventually, whatever I'd be expecting would turn into a reality –all thanks to my self-fulfilling prophecies!

It is very easy to point the finger at others or blame the world for our problems. But when we dare to look deep inside, it becomes obvious that all the problems in the outside world manifest from our own subconscious mind. The outside world serves as a perfect mirror to our inner world. If you can't convince your subconscious mind that you are worthy and deserving of what you desire, then what you want is going to continue eluding you in the external world.

Again, how you talk to yourself and about yourself will give you a better understanding of how you perceive your self-worth. Trust me, you are perfectly worthy and deserving of all that you desire. You just have to start believing it! It's okay if right now you have no idea how to make it happen.

Just the fact that you have picked this book up and you are reading it right now demonstrates that you are ready for a change. I truly commend you for this. Most people say they want to change their life, but they never take any action to make it happen. You are already doing well because you are truly willing to make the desired changes. Stay committed – I promise you won't be the same person by the end of this book, provided you'd do all the exercises and put into action everything I am sharing with you.

Knowing, Understanding, and Prioritizing Your Own Needs

Most people are so out of touch with themselves that they don't even know what their needs are. If you are one of them, then it is time to start focusing on developing greater self-awareness. To live a fulfilling life, you have to know what your physical, mental, emotional, and spiritual needs are.

Every day, you must intentionally cater to your body, mind, and soul. This means prioritizing your "me-time." If you aren't already scheduling any "me-time" into your day, then it is high time that you start doing it.

What it looks like in practice differs from person to person, but the essence of scheduled "me time" is that you must spend time looking after your body, mind, and soul. This could mean engaging in some form of physical exercise, meditation, breathwork, reading, practicing affirmations, etc.

You don't have to do all of these things every day. You can pick a few that you resonate with and add them to your daily routine. Just make sure that you are doing at least one activity every day for all three aspects of your being: mind, body, and soul. Stay committed to doing things that energize you and help you recharge your batteries.

You can also schedule different activities for different days if you are someone who thrives on variety. As I said earlier, every single day, you must schedule the time to look after your body, mind, and soul. This shouldn't feel like work. It should feel refreshing and something that you look forward to doing every day. The idea may seem overwhelming right now if you already have an over-packed schedule, but you must get started.

Also, if you have so much on your plate that you are constantly feeling overwhelmed, then it is time to start prioritizing your tasks more efficiently. Start delegating what you can to others. For instance, ask your children to help lay the table so that you can serve dinner faster.

At work, don't shy away from asking for help from a colleague who can help you complete your tasks better. Most of the time we don't receive the help we want because we never ask for it. Trust me, your loved ones want to lighten your burden. But for that, you must tell them exactly how they can help you out.

If you think you have to do everything yourself because no one can do everything as well as you can, then that's a different kind of issue. You have to let go of your perfectionism if you want to be happy in life. So many people overload their platter by taking up more responsibilities than they are realistically able to handle.

Remembering to practice Pareto's Principle really helps me in this case. It is so true that only 20% of the things create 80% of the results (Wikipedia, n.d.). Busyness doesn't indicate productivity. You have to become really good at identifying those 20% things that contribute to 80% of your results. Once you start focusing on doing more high-impact activities and fewer low-impact activities that don't contribute much towards your goals, it gets easier to delegate tasks to others.

There are only 24 hours in a day. You just can't afford to keep running around in circles like a hamster on a wheel. It is absolutely crucial that you take the time to look after yourself. You deserve your own love and care. You should spend at least 1-2 hours every day taking care of yourself physically, mentally, emotionally, and spiritually. You are worth it!

SELF-LOVE QUIZ

I have designed this quiz to help you understand how committed you are to self-love. Even if you get a low score, I would urge you to not feel bad about it. This quiz is not a measure of your self-worth but of the degree of self-love you have. It is okay if you don't have enough self-love right now.

This book is about radical unconditional self-love which means you are willing to accept and love yourself in spite of all your perceived and real imperfections. So if currently you don't have a lot of self-love in your heart, it is okay - you must accept yourself exactly the way you are right now.

A quiz like this helps you gain perspective. You'd know which areas you are weakest in and, hence, you can work on strengthening yourself in those areas. The questions where you scored the lowest will show you your areas of weakness. Make a special note of these and then dedicatedly work on improving yourself in these areas.

I would strongly recommend that you take this quiz twice - once at the beginning of your journey and again after completing chapter eight. Make note of your initial score. It would be fascinating to observe how far you'd have come by the end of the eighth chapter.

For each question, give yourself a score on a scale of 0-4. This is what each number indicates: 0 = strongly disagree, 1 = disagree, 2 = neutral, 3 = agree, 4 = strongly agree. Use the scoring guide at the end of this quiz to understand your results.

1. When you look in the mirror, you feel good about your body. _____
2. You forgive yourself for the mistakes you have made. _____
3. You enjoy your own company when no one is around. _____
4. You like taking care of yourself. _____

5. You regularly make time for self-care. ____
6. You are proud of who you are. ____
7. You don't take other people's criticism of you personally. ____
8. You believe in yourself. ____
9. You trust that you can achieve any goal you set your mind upon. ____
10. You feel you are a lovable person. ____
11. You rarely ever feel the blues. ____
12. You love your life. ____
13. You trust your judgment and decisions. ____
14. You are committed to personal development. ____
15. You are always looking for ways to be better. ____
16. You know how to love yourself while also aspiring to be an even better version of yourself. ____
17. You talk positively about yourself to others. ____
18. Your self-talk with yourself is positive, uplifting, and encouraging. ____
19. You feel comfortable saying 'no' to things you don't want to do. ____
20. You never allow anyone to trample your boundaries. ____
21. You are very good at delegating the less important tasks to others. ____
22. You regularly do things that help you feel renewed and refreshed. ____
23. You love and accept yourself unconditionally with all your perfections and imperfections. ____

24. You know that your presence adds value to other people's lives. _____
25. You know that you are a valuable person. _____
26. You always know what's best for you. _____
27. You are kind to yourself. _____
28. You know your voice and your opinions are important. _____
29. You are assertive when it comes to establishing and maintaining your boundaries. _____
30. You feel comfortable being yourself around others. _____

Your Total Score: _____

SCORING GUIDE

Use this guide to understand your results.

100-120 – You really do love yourself! This is wonderful. This book will help you develop even greater self-love. Love, after all, is a verb. The more positive actions you take to cultivate self-love, the better your life is going to be. You are on the right path.

You are already doing well. The questions where you scored slightly low will indicate to you those areas where you can improve even further. Stay committed to self-love. Always remember that no matter how far you have come, there is always another level you can reach!

70-100 – You do love yourself to a certain extent but there are areas where improvement is needed. This is wonderful news because if you are doing well in certain areas, then it shouldn't be too hard to improve in other areas. The questions where you scored slightly low will indicate to you those areas that you should focus on in this journey of self-improvement.

You are going to benefit greatly from this book as we are going to discuss many practical ideas that you can use to cultivate deeper self-love. If you'll do everything I am going to share with you, then you'll definitely have a different score by the time you finish this workbook.

>70 – You are in the right place. It is okay if you are struggling with self-love. The fact that you have picked this book up shows how committed you are to changing your life. You just need the right guidance, and that's something this book is going to provide you with. I would urge you to remain committed to this journey. Do all the exercises in this book with due diligence. Take the time to mull over the wisdom encapsulated in each chapter.

Think about how you can immediately put into practice what you are learning. Whenever you start feeling engulfed by the clouds of self-doubt, reaffirm to yourself, "I am committed to self-love. I am worthy and deserving of love and acceptance." Practice this affirmation as frequently as you need to and also use it to fill moments of silence when your mind beings wandering aimlessly here and there. Stay on this journey, and you'll definitely be a different person by the end of chapter eight!

2

RADICAL SELF-LOVE BEGINS WITH RADICAL SELF-ACCEPTANCE

"Self-love has very little to do with how you feel about your outer self. It's about accepting all of yourself."

— TYRA BANKS

R adical self-love begins with radical self-acceptance. You cannot love yourself in the truest sense of the word without first accepting yourself completely. Indeed, I am talking about accepting yourself exactly the way you are – with all your positive and negative qualities.

You cannot put off practicing self-love until another day when you'll be a better version of yourself. You have to love who you are right now. There is nothing worse than giving yourself a shifting goal post putting off self-love for another place and time. I did it to myself for years so I know exactly how that feels. I stopped aiming for perfection only once I realized a profound truth about human life. No matter how far you come in life, there is always another level to aspire to. Perfection is an illusion that can never be attained – it is much better to strive for excellence instead.

Life can never be fulfilling without self-love. If you think you can start focusing on self-love once you have achieved your goals or when you are a better person than who you are today, it's never going to happen. This is akin to an over-weight person saying they will start exercising once they have lost 50 pounds. It just doesn't happen!

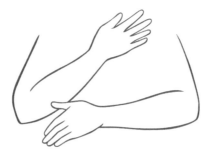

Your struggles with self-love are closely related to your lack of self-acceptance. The irony is that we want others to accept us for who we are when we repeatedly fail to accept ourselves for who we are. Again, I want to emphasize the fact that no one can give you what you are not giving to yourself. If you want others to accept you fully for who you are, you must commit to self-acceptance first.

In my past relationships, I used to get very upset and disappointed because my partners wouldn't accept me for who I am. They would constantly try to change me and put me down by being hypercritical of me. Blaming them for being unkind and inconsiderate was the easy thing to do, but when I sat down to really look within, I realized that they were showing me a reflection of my own relationship with myself. How could I expect someone else to accept me when I was not accepting myself for who I was?

Also, because I was so broken inside and desperate for love, I was attracting and feeling attracted to people who didn't love themselves. Since they were lacking in self-love, they were also struggling with self-acceptance. As I said earlier, no one can accept another human being unless they learn to fully accept their own self first.

There is really nothing worse than two broken people trying to have a relationship together. It is doomed to be dysfunctional because both parties are trying to extract out of the other person something they are not capable of giving to themselves. I didn't accept myself so my partners didn't accept me for who I was. While I was busy complaining about their lack of acceptance towards me, I failed to realize another profound truth: I wasn't able to accept them for who they were either!

Think about it – if I was being truly accepting of them would I complain and crib so much about how they were making me feel? If you want to have a peaceful and fulfilling relationship with another human being, then you have to accept them exactly the way they are. No matter how hard it is for you to accept this fact, the truth is you cannot change another human being. The harder you try, the worse your relationship is going to get because no one wants to feel forced to change for someone else's sake. If you are currently guilty of this, then stop, please!

Now, I am not suggesting that you should be a doormat in your relationship with others and accept however badly they may choose to treat you. Of course, not! Authentic self-love is all about having strong boundaries. You have to say 'no' and walk away when your needs are not being met in a relationship or when a relationship is draining you in some way.

Real self-love is the ability to be comfortable with yourself and perfectly happy in your own company. When you are content with yourself, you stop getting into relationships out of the fear of being alone. You love yourself too much for it. If you aren't there yet, then don't worry, you will get there. Trust me, the fact that you are reading this book and doing all the exercises tells me, you are committed to self-improvement.

Success is all about showing up. No matter how far out of reach the goal may seem, for now, you'll definitely achieve it provided you remain committed to the path and keep doing the work. Moving forward, complete and unconditional self-acceptance should be your motto.

WHERE DOES LACK OF SELF-ACCEPTANCE COME FROM

Our early life experiences have a powerful impact on who we become as adults. If our parents didn't make us feel unconditionally accepted for who we were as children, it is inevitable that we'll struggle with self-love in our adult life. I am not saying this so that you can place the blame on your parents and not take full responsibility for your lack of self-love and self-acceptance. That would be extremely disem-powering!

No matter what happened in your life, you have to take full responsibility for who you are right now and for everything that you have or don't have in your life. Taking responsibility doesn't mean you have to blame yourself for all the unfortu-nate things that have happened in your life. It simply means you are ready to claim your power to rise above the past. Who you want to be and how you want to live your life is entirely in your own hands. You are the only one who has the power to choose your present and your future. You can either be a victim or the master of your destiny – it is your choice entirely!

It took me a long time to get out of the victim mindset. I spent a lot of time blaming my parents and my early life experiences for the things that weren't going well for me. Nothing good came out of it. I just kept wallowing in the cesspool of self-pity. Eventually, I had one very profound realization. I was operating from the perspective that my parents are supposed to be perfect because they are my parents. Society plants this idea in our minds that parents are supposed to have all the answers. Just because they have given birth to children, they must have all of life figured out. In reality, this is hardly ever the case.

Accept yourself

When I started thinking of my parents as fellow human beings on a similar journey as mine, I stopped having such expectations. I realized that they did the best that they were capable of based on the knowledge and understanding they had. In their flawed ways, they tried to do the best for me. I also realized that their inability to accept me was rooted in their lack of self-acceptance. In fact, this is true for everyone. It takes a tremendous amount of self-awareness and an intense commitment to self-improvement to foster that kind of radical self-acceptance. Most people fail miserably at it so we can't blame them for not giving us what they aren't able to give to themselves.

Besides, not everyone is interested in self-improvement the way you and I are. The fact that I am writing this book for you and you are reading it shows that we both have an intense desire to be better versions of ourselves. I am sharing what I have learned in my own journey of self-evolution and you are learning from it so that you can create similar results for yourself. It is important to keep in mind that not everyone thinks like this. Most people want to remain confined to their comfort zone. It is not our responsibility or even our right to judge their journey no matter how close we are to them.

My parents didn't know any better when they made me feel less than accepted for who I was. Chances are that's how their parents treated them as well. It is also likely that's how their parents' parents treated their parents. The cycle of misery gets passed on from one generation to another until someone intentionally decides to break it. Since you are reading this book, you can become that person for your family.

You have empowered yourself with the understanding that to truly accept another human being, you have to accept yourself first. Hence, you have also developed the ability to give to others what you may not have received from them. Keep your cup so full with radical self-acceptance and self-love that you can easily share your abundance with others.

Something miraculous happens once we begin practicing radical self-acceptance and self-love. The people who were hypercritical of us either start distancing themselves from us or they may even disappear from our lives. We also start attracting new people into our lives who accept and love us unconditionally.

It is also possible that our existing relationships may undergo a complete transformation. Others may suddenly become a lot more accepting and loving towards you. It happens because the external world is truly a mirror of our inner world. Unlike what most people believe, real transformation is always an inside-out process. You cannot change anything in your life without first transforming your own self in some way.

FORGIVENESS IS ESSENTIAL FOR ACCEPTANCE

You must forgive your parents for the things they didn't do right – they just didn't know any better. But first, you must forgive yourself for the things you yourself didn't do right. It is okay to be imperfect. It is okay to not get everything right all the time. It is okay to make mistakes. Your past doesn't have to be a life sentence – learn from it and let it go.

Human beings are not supposed to be perfect. You must let go of this idea that there is something wrong with you because you have flaws and shortcomings. Trust me, there isn't a single person on this planet right now who isn't imperfect in some way. No matter how perfect someone may look, every single person on this planet is deeply flawed.

Owning your flaws and shortcomings is extremely empowering. Magic happens once you stop criticizing yourself for not being perfect. When you stop demanding perfection from your own self, you also stop expecting it from others.

Forgive yourself for all your mistakes - learn from them but don't let them hold you hostage. When you forgive yourself, it gets easier to forgive others. Remember, you can never give to someone else what you don't have for yourself. To forgive your parents and everyone else in your life, you must start by forgiving yourself first.

EXERCISE

Set an hour or two aside and write a letter of forgiveness to yourself. Address this letter to yourself as if you were writing the letter to your best friend. In other words, be just as kind and thoughtful towards yourself as you would be towards your best friend. While writing the letter, think of what you would say to your best friend who has been feeling guilty about past mistakes. You deserve to hear such kind and encouraging words just as much as your best friend does.

Writing this forgiveness letter is often an extremely cathartic process. Once you shift your perspective and start seeing yourself as your best friend, you suddenly realize just how hard you have been on yourself all this time. You deserve to be treated better. The journey to greater self-love begins with forgiveness.

Forgive yourself for all your past mistakes – you did things the way you did because you simply didn't know any better. Now, you have evolved into a finer version of yourself. Moving forward, you'll do everything better. Learn from the past but let go of it. Take your time to write this letter as thoroughly as possible. You can also set aside an entire day for doing it. Write down every single mistake and fully express all the negative emotions you have been holding on to.

I would recommend that you do this exercise in a peaceful place. Turn your phone off and let your family know you are going to need some time by yourself. Request them to not disturb you unless it was an emergency. No matter how busy you are and how many responsibilities you have to fulfill, you deserve some time by yourself. Ask for help from others so that they can take charge of **your** duties while you take this time to work on yourself.

You can also play some soft music in the background and light a few candles to help create a relaxing atmosphere. Allow yourself to feel all the emotions that come up during this process. Don't try to suppress them. Let them rise fully – own them, accept them, embrace them. No emotion is bad.

Every emotion is there to help us experience the full spectrum of human life. We cannot embrace happiness without also embracing sadness. We cannot embrace joy without also embracing pain. We are taught from an early age that certain emotions are bad. We begin suppressing these emotions. That's how emotional and psychological issues take root in our consciousness.

Once we start fully accepting all our emotions, the negative ones stop having so much power over us. Always remember: what you resist, persists. The best way to make yourself feel an emotion at its full intensity is by striving to not feel it at all. By trying to resist something, you give your power to it.

Instead, embrace all the emotions that are arising in your consciousness. Allow yourself to revisit and relive the past. IT IS OKAY THAT YOU WERE NOT PERFECT AND IT IS OKAY THAT YOU ARE NOT PERFECT NOW. Give up this burden of perfection. If you have learned from the past and you are striving to be better today, then you are doing well.

After writing the letter, you can burn it and release the ashes into a flowing water body. If you don't have access to a flowing water body, then you can also flush the ashes. If you don't want to burn the letter, then you can also make small pieces of it and bury it in the earth. The point is to release and let go of all that you have held onto for so long. After completing the release ritual, you'll experience an immediate shift. You'll feel lighter – as if a load has been lifted of your shoulders.

SELF-ACCEPTANCE QUIZ

After completing the letter-writing exercise, come back here and take this self-acceptance quiz. If you haven't done the letter-writing exercise yet, then I would advise you to go back and do that first. You would definitely experience a massive shift, and when you get back to taking this quiz, the results would be a lot more encouraging.

Again, the point of this quiz is not to make you feel about where you are in life right now. The purpose of this quiz is to help you better understand where you currently are on the self-acceptance spectrum. Knowledge is power. By having a thorough understanding of where you are right now, you can steer your efforts in the right direction. The areas where you score the lowest are the areas that need your maximum attention.

No matter what your score turns out to be, accept and embrace your results. You are perfect the way you are no matter what the scores say. Self-acceptance isn't about embracing a mythical perfect version of yourself. It is all about fully owning and embracing yourself exactly the way you are.

Lastly, keep in mind that self-love and self-acceptance aren't traits we are born with. They are skills anyone can develop with intentional practice. The fact that you are reading this book and doing these exercises tells me you are committed to developing these skills. Stay committed – you'll definitely get the results!

For each question, give yourself a score on a scale of 0-4. This is what each number indicates: 0 = strongly disagree, 1 = disagree, 2 = neutral, 3 = agree, 4 = strongly agree. Use the scoring guide at the end of this quiz to understand your results.

1. I know who I am. ____
2. I am perfectly lovable exactly the way I am. ____
3. I allow others to love me. ____
4. It is easy for me to be kind to myself. ____
5. I am very good at taking care of myself. ____
6. I enjoy looking after myself. ____
7. I truly believe that it is okay to be imperfect. ____

8. I forgive myself for my mistakes. ____
9. I understand that I am imperfect just like everyone else in this world. ____
10. My imperfections make me unique and charming. ____
11. I am a valuable human being. ____
12. It is easy for me to be honest with myself. ____
13. Most of the time, I take full responsibility for my life and my own actions. ____
14. I don't bash myself for my mistakes. I learn from them and release them quickly. ____
15. I rarely indulge in self-sabotaging behavior (like over-eating, overspending, constantly looking for signs of cheating in a relationship, etc.). ____
16. I trust I can handle anything that comes my way. ____
17. I trust the process of life. ____
18. I am grateful for my past because it has made me who I am today. ____
19. I have no regrets in life. ____
20. I am proud of the life I have lived so far. ____
21. I feel blessed. ____
22. My destiny is in my own hands. ____
23. I know my strengths. ____
24. I know how to use my strengths to create favorable results. ____
25. I know what my weaknesses are. ____

26. I believe I can turn my weaknesses into strengths.

    ____

27. I own myself completely and unconditionally. ____

28. I love all aspects of myself. ____

29. Most of the time, I live in the here and now. ____

30. I am not a prisoner of my past. ____

Your Total Score: _____

SCORING GUIDE

Use this guide to understand your results.

100-120 – You are doing well! Self-acceptance is an art you have mastered to a great extent. Keep practicing self-acceptance and self-love. Growth is a never-ending process. You can always raise yourself to an even higher level of authentic self-love and self-acceptance. Make a note of those places where you scored the lowest. In the next exercise, I will show you how to take your game to a whole different level!

70-100 – You do accept yourself to a certain extent. With practice, you can increase your level of self-acceptance. Go back to your score sheet and observe where you scored the lowest. Make a note of those statements. In the next exercise, I will show you how to convert these negative statements into positive affirmations. Again, self-acceptance and self-love are skills we develop and not traits we are born with. The more you practice, the better you are going to get it.

>70 – I know you are struggling with self-acceptance. IT IS OKAY! You don't have to bash yourself for your scores on this quiz. This score is not a reflection of your worth as a human being. You are a valuable and wonderful human being who deserves the very best. Accept yourself for who you are right now. By doing just this, your life will begin to change for the better. Self-acceptance means you are ready and willing to accept every single aspect of your being. This includes the fact that you struggle with self-acceptance. You'll soon realize that it all becomes less of a struggle once you start embracing everything instead of resisting it.

EXERCISE – AFFIRMATIONS

Positive affirmations are a perfect tool for counteracting negative self-talk. I want you to go back to the previous exercise and pick all the statements where you received a low score. For instance, let us assume that you scored really low on this statement: "I believe I can turn my weaknesses into strengths."

Now, turn this into a positive affirmation by writing it in the present tense as if it were already true for you. This is what it would look like, "I have mastered the art of turning my weaknesses into strengths."

Here's another example for the same statement: "I feel blessed." You can turn this into an affirmation like this: "I love how blessed I feel every single day of my life."

Be sure to write your affirmations in the present tense as if what you are affirming is already an established truth in your life. Moving forward, whenever you start feeling negative, go back to these affirmations and read them out aloud or in your mind. Also, get in the habit of reading them every morning and evening at least seven times. Ideally, you'd want to read them a minimum 21 times every morning and evening.

The best time for practicing affirmations is early in the morning immediately after you get out of bed and at night right before you fall asleep. At these two times of the day, the doorways of the subconscious mind are wide open. Since your subconscious mind creates your reality, you can transform your life only by transfiguring your subconscious blueprint. Affirmations are a perfect tool for this purpose.

The more frequently you practice an affirmation, the more strongly it becomes rooted in your subconscious mind. Hence, the more strongly it impacts your life. I want to give you another powerful affirmation that you can add to your daily routine. Chant it as frequently as you can. Here it is:

"I love myself wholly, completely, and unconditionally. I accept myself wholly, completely, and unconditionally. I am perfect exactly the way I am. I am worthy and deserving of all that is best and wonderful."

Chant this affirmation as frequently as possible. Also, add it to your morning and evening routine. For more life-transforming affirmations, you can check out my *I am Capable of Anything* series where I have shared unique affirmations that can be practiced three times a day.

3

APPRECIATE YOURSELF

"When you undervalue what you do, the world will undervalue who you are."

— OPRAH WINFREY

When was the last **time** you patted yourself on the back and said, "Well done!" If you are like most people, then most likely, you **don't** remember when you did this, or worse still, you have **perhaps** never done it at all.

If you find it hard to appreciate yourself, then I don't blame you at all. It isn't the norm in society. From an early age, we are encouraged to seek approval and appreciation from others. We are taught that to **be** "good" we have to do exactly what pleases our parents, teachers, and other authority figures. Hence, it is not surprising that our sense of self-worth becomes tied to the acceptance and approval of others.

LOVE YOURSELF

The problem is that our parents, teachers, and other authority figures are also flawed human beings. Not everything we learned from them consciously or subconsciously is good for us or supports our highest good. As adults, we must do a lot of unlearning if we want to be genuinely happy and live up to our fullest potential.

Seeking acceptance and approval from others compels you to shift your locus of control outside of yourself. Since you cannot control how others see or treat you, you start feeling like a victim of circumstances. Self-acceptance and self-appreciation help you maintain an internal locus of control.

You aren't relying on others to give you what you need. Instead, you learn to give yourself exactly what you need. Once you learn to fulfill your own needs, you become a formidable force of nature. Self-love makes you indestructible. No one can harm a person who is rooted in deep unconditional self-love.

COME TO TERMS WITH YOUR INNER CRITIC

Have you ever seen a baby indulge in self-loathing? I am sure your answer is going to be a resounding "No." Isn't it interesting that we have all been that baby at some point completely in love with ourselves? Yet by the time we grew up, the voice of the inner critic became extremely strong and overpowering.

This inner critic tells you "You are not capable" "You are not worthy" "You don't deserve this" and a million other things that disempower you. It is very hard to silence this inner critic because it seems to yell at you every step of the way. Every time you start making the effort to move beyond the past and create positive changes in your life, it pulls you back.

As a result, you remain stuck in a vicious cycle of feeling unworthy and undeserving. The first step towards conquering and silencing the inner critic involves becoming aware that this voice isn't yours. You internalized this voice based on the criticism and comments you heard from the authority figures in your life while growing up.

Once you start recognizing the fact that this voice isn't yours, it becomes easier to start distancing yourself from it. Whatever this voice is telling you isn't your own truth, but instead, it is someone else's opinion of you. Opinions, as we all know, are biased and flawed.

You don't have to live the rest of your life inside the prison of someone else's opinion. As a child, you didn't have much power over what was told to you. But as an adult, you can enforce strong boundaries and show others how to treat you. Most of all, you have the power to free yourself from the prison of the past. The people in your life didn't know any better but now you can choose to not be affected by their opinions and biases.

What you were told growing up wasn't the fact of your life or of who you are – it was a projection of someone else's reality. Others will say you are incapable of something when, in reality, they believe they are the ones who are incapable of it.

The same applies to all negative ideas and beliefs you were imparted as a child. It is a reflection of someone else's limited worldview. You don't have to accept it. This is why I always say that self-awareness is the first and the most important step in the journey of personal transformation. By being self-aware, you can start distancing yourself from the inner critic that sabotages your growth. That nagging voice inside your head isn't your own voice, and it is certainly not spouting facts at you. It is someone else's voice that has become internalized in your subconscious mind. To progress in life, you must get rid of it.

The best part is that the subconscious mind is programmable. Just like how you can erase old data and write new data on your computer, you can do the same with the subconscious mind. Your conscious mind is that part of your consciousness which remains actively aware of what you are thinking. However, this part of the mind is like the tip of an iceberg – it is very limited in capacity and has only so much influence over your life.

The subconscious mind is that part of your consciousness that almost entirely determines and influences your reality. It is a massive data bank where all your beliefs, ideas, and memories are stored. The interesting thing is that even the things that you think you have forgotten about are never really forgotten by the subconscious mind.

You may think you have eliminated a negative experience from your memory by not thinking about it, but the subconscious never forgets anything. It remembers everything until you go back and rewrite what has become imprinted. For that, you need to consciously use tools like meditation, affirmations, incantations, breathwork, etc. In this book, we'll be using many of these tools to erase negative programming from your subconscious mind.

I am sharing all this with you to help you come to terms with your past. It is important to understand that if you had an overly critical parent growing up, their harshness towards you was a projection of their lack of self-love. Their criticism of you was an extension of their lack of acceptance towards their own self.

As an adult, you may have distanced yourself from that hypercritical parent, and you consciously try to not remember all the painful things they said to you. But the real problem is that their harsh words have become internalized in your subconscious mind. You aren't vigilant of it like you are of your parent in the external world because at a very deep level you have begun to identify that nagging voice inside your mind as your own.

This is also the reason why you may say you want something at the conscious level but your actions and your beliefs don't match that reality. For instance, as I shared earlier, I really thought there was nothing I wanted more badly than a relationship. But every time I got involved with someone, I found ways to sabotage that relationship. I would start hunting for signs of infidelity or for them to leave me until that expectation would become my reality.

What you say or think at the level of the conscious mind has very little value unless you learn to bring your subconscious mind in alignment with it. After all, your thoughts, behavior, and actions are determined by your subconscious mind. This can be done only by intentionally fostering and practicing deep self-awareness.

EXERCISE

Take some time to reflect on what that inner critic is telling you right now. Note down everything it is saying in the space provided below. If you start running short of space, use a notebook or diary to record all your thoughts and emotions.

Moving forward I want you to carry a notebook with you everywhere you go. You can also use a digital diary if you don't want to carry a physical notebook with you. Whenever you start hearing the voice of the inner critic, pull out this diary and start writing everything it is telling you. By simply writing things down, you'll kickstart the process of disassociating from this voice. This practice will also help you practice deeper self-awareness.

At the end of the week, go through everything you have written down. You'll be amazed to notice that before you wrote things down it seemed as if there were a million thoughts in your head. When you look at them in a written format, you realize there are only a handful of thoughts that your mind keeps repeating over and over again. Because of the frequency with which the same or similar thoughts occur, you feel overwhelmed. You feel there are too many thoughts on your mind, but in reality, thoughts are often repeated in patterns.

Once you have identified your thought patterns, you can create your own positive affirmations that counteract the negative thought patterns. Go back to the previous chapter and read the exercise on affirmation creation and practice, if you need to. Moving forward, whenever negative thoughts start pestering you again, replace them with positive affirmations. Repeat these affirmations as frequently as possible. Over time, your mind will begin to accept them as your new reality, but you must persist in your efforts if you want to get results.

TAKE PRIDE IN YOUR ACCOMPLISHMENTS

For most of us while we were growing up nothing we ever did felt good enough. We were told that we need to do better no matter how good our grades turned out or how hard we worked. Our accomplishments were hardly ever celebrated, but our failures or shortcomings were always harshly criticized.

Unfortunately, we end up carrying this attitude into our adult life constantly belittling and being dismissive of our own accomplishments while holding on too tightly to all our real and perceived failures.

From now on, I want you to shift your perspective. Instead of focusing on your failures start celebrating your accomplishments. Of course, you should learn from setbacks and failures, but never allow them to hold you back. You don't have to be a prisoner of your past for the rest of your life. The gate is wide open – you can choose to walk out of this life sentence that so many of us give to ourselves in ignorance.

People often erroneously think that criticism and constant chiding help in achieving goals. Just imagine a beautiful baby in front of you. Every time this baby started walking in wobbly steps and fell down, you'd start scolding the baby harshly. What will happen to that baby? Won't it be utterly cruel to do that? Maybe that baby would even start believing that he was simply not capable of walking and would give up altogether.

But you have a heart – you'll never do this to a baby. My question is why are you doing this to yourself? Why do you expect yourself to do everything perfectly when you are learning something new? Why do you have to treat yourself so harshly? I am sure that if the baby was in front of you right now attempting to take his first steps forward, you'll cheer on the baby. You have to start doing the same for yourself. Start appreciating yourself for the efforts you are putting in, even if you don't get the desired results straight away.

"I would praise you, but
your value is beyond words."

Reward is a much better teacher than punishment. Once you start celebrating your accomplishments, you'll also automatically manifest more reasons to celebrate. Your ability to create results is closely tied to your self-image and your beliefs about yourself. You have to train yourself to see the best in yourself.

You are worthy of your own appreciation and encouragement. Don't let anyone tell you otherwise. You are an incredible human being who deserves the very best. You just have to start treating yourself like you would treat a beautiful baby who was learning to walk. Cheer on yourself, and celebrate all your wins – both big and small.

EXERCISE

In the space below, write down at least 10 major accomplishments you have had that you are proud of. It doesn't necessarily have to be something that is deemed a major achievement by society at large. If it was something significant for you, then it is worth acknowledging and celebrating! For instance, getting back in shape, recovering from a major setback, or anything else that felt like a significant achievement to you should be included in this list.

No achievement is ever too small to be acknowledged and celebrated. When you were feeling low and emotionally distressed, maybe your greatest achievement was simply getting out of bed and getting dressed for the day. It is worth acknowledging and celebrating such an achievement as well.

Get in the habit of recognizing and celebrating all your accomplishments. The more frequently you do this, the more feathers you'll add to your cap!

_____

_____

_____

_____

_____

_____

REWARD YOURSELF GENEROUSLY

If it is important to do loving and caring things for others, then it is all the more important to do those things for yourself. As I said earlier, reward is a much better teacher than punishment. We are all very good at punishing ourselves. Unfortunately, rewarding ourselves isn't something that we think about so much. Just imagine – when was the last time you gave yourself a gift or some kind of reward for your achievements?

More often than not, the answer I receive is "Never!" I am sure if I asked you about the last time you scolded yourself or punished yourself in some way, it won't be that hard to recall that instance. It's alright, though! No one teaches us these things growing up. You are learning something new – it's okay if you don't have a lot of experience doing it so far. Through practice, you can master any habit.

You must appreciate yourself for the commitment you have made to change your life for the better. You are reading this book because you are open to the idea of practicing radical self-love and self-acceptance. Simply being open to this possibility is a significant achievement in its own right.

From now on, I want you to reward yourself regularly for everything you are doing well. Something incredible will happen once you start doing this. You'll be amazed to realize how many things you are already doing well. It's just that you have been so focused on the negative that it seemed like the list of things you weren't doing right was far longer than the list of things you are doing right.

This is generally the case for most people. Once you start writing down all your accomplishments regularly, you start observing that most of the time you are doing well. A shift in perspective is often a lot more important than an immediate change of circumstances. The latter comes a lot more easily once the former is taken care of.

Moving forward, I want you to not just recognize and acknowledge your accomplishments but also celebrate them. Every time you do something that requires you to move outside of your comfort zone or that feels like an important step in the right direction, I want you to reward yourself.

This reward should be something that you really enjoy or cherish having. For instance, a massage, or a favorite meal, and if it is within your budget, then maybe you can also purchase that item you have had on your wishlist for a long time now.

By rewarding yourself for all the good things you are doing, you train yourself to do more of those things that are worth celebrating. Punishment works in the same way. By chiding and punishing yourself for the things you are not doing right, you actually train yourself to do more of those undesirable things. Hence, choose wisely!

EXERCISE

Go back to the previous section where you wrote down your accomplishments. Next to each accomplishment, write down a reward you are going to give yourself. In the next few weeks, let yourself enjoy these rewards.

From now on, get in the habit of acknowledging your successes. Keep a diary handy for noting down all your big and small achievements. Every time you note down an accomplishment, be sure to reward yourself for it. Rewards can be both big and small.

Ideally, it should be proportionate to the size of your accomplishment. For instance, the reward for going to the gym every day for 7 days can be allowing yourself to have a healthy dessert once a week. When you accomplish something big, give yourself a massive reward for it!

I would suggest that you create a list of everything you enjoy doing in a separate notebook, and then, pick something from there to add to your accomplishment journal every time you hit a goalpost.

For starters, write down 20 things here that you enjoy doing the most. You can pick items from this list to add next to your accomplishments in the previous section. You deserve these rewards!

REALIZE THAT YOU ARE NOT THE ONLY ONE WHO IS IMPERFECT

We judge ourselves way too harshly by comparing ourselves with others. We look at the accomplishments of others and compare our weaknesses with their strengths. It's a skewed and unfair comparison that can only cause unhappiness and dissatisfaction.

You must realize that every human being on this planet is imperfect. It may seem like some people have everything figured out, but there really isn't a single human being on this planet who isn't struggling with something or the other. Our strengths and weaknesses are distinct to us. Hence, the nature of our struggles is also different. But I can assure you of one thing – no one is perfect!

Besides, there are certain things that every single human being struggles with. For instance, laziness is one of those things that we all have a propensity for. Of course, the definition of laziness can differ from person to person, but more often than not, we all feel we aren't living up to our full potential. There is something really freeing about having this realization. Once you realize that your struggles aren't something exclusive to you, it becomes easier to accept that there is nothing wrong with you.

You can be kinder and more compassionate to yourself when you understand that a lot of the things you struggle with are part and parcel of the human experience. Every human being has to face their inner demons in order to rise to their full potential. Instead of chiding yourself for where you are falling short, keep your focus on encouraging yourself where you are thriving. If you can get in the habit of doing this, then, eventually, you'll master the art of turning your weaknesses into strengths.

EXERCISE

Research the life of someone you admire. If it is a famous person, then try to read their interviews, books, podcasts, or any other material you can find. Delve deep into understanding what they have struggled with and how they overcame their challenges. It is easy to look at the veneer of success and allow yourself to be bewitched by it. You must understand that they got where they are by overcoming hardships and fighting their inner demons.

If this is a person you know in real life, then you can spend some time with them. Ask them introspective questions to learn about their struggles and how they got to where they are.

In the space below, you can write down some of the things this individual has struggled with and a summary of how they overcame it. This will help you realize that they are not that different from you. If they can do it, then so can you!

_____

_____

_____

_____

_____

_____

_____

_____

_____

_____

_____

_____

_____

RECEIVE APPRECIATION GRACIOUSLY

We are taught to give generously, but most of us never learn how to receive graciously. Giving and receiving are two sides of the same coin. If you are only giving and never allowing yourself to receive, then you'll never experience authentic fulfillment. To balance the scale, you must open yourself up to receive more. This gives the people in your life a chance to express their love and care to you.

If you are someone who never accepts help, it is time to make some changes. You don't have to do everything by yourself – it is okay to receive. In fact, receiving graciously can be a deeply enriching experience for both the giver and the receiver. By rejecting the gift someone else wants to give you, you are depriving them of a chance to express their love and care to you.

I want you to start becoming comfortable with receiving the gifts that others want to give you from their heart – both material and energetic. So the next time someone pays you a compliment, don't counteract it by putting yourself down. Instead, just say "thank you." If someone is sincerely paying you a compliment, then that means they are acknowledging and honoring the beauty of your soul.

Counteracting it by putting yourself down is akin to throwing a beautifully wrapped present back at the giver. Would you do it to someone if it was an actual present they handed over to you? Compliments and sincere appreciation are beautifully wrapped gifts. Hold them close to your heart and respond with a simple "thank you" from now on.

Also, be open to receiving material gifts and help of any kind that another person wants to provide you with. If they are doing it from their heart, then it is again a beautifully wrapped present that you wouldn't want to throw back at them.

EXERCISE

For practice, ask a loved one to compliment you today. Visualize that you are receiving a present from them – allow yourself to receive it fully. All you need to say is a simple "thank you" along with a beautiful smile on your face. You must let yourself feel worthy of what you are receiving.

From now on, if someone pays you a compliment, always reply with a simple "thank you." It would help to visualize that they are handing you a beautifully wrapped present – accept it and hold it close to your heart. Never throw it back to them by counteracting it.

4

SPEND TIME WITH YOURSELF

"*Spending time alone in your own company reinforces your self-worth and is often the number-one way to replenish your resilience reserves.*"

— SAM OWEN

We live in a society where distraction is encouraged and spending time alone in quiet reflection is frowned upon. Thanks to the modern world, we have an overabundance of tools to distract ourselves with. If you'll only observe how most people live their lives, you'll realize that they are constantly jumping from one tool of distraction to another.

In fact, the vast majority of modern parents hand over a mobile phone to their children instead of playing with them or getting them engaged in more meaningful activities. The point I am trying to make here is that we live in a society where spending time by yourself isn't considered a priority. To a large extent, solitude and silence are frowned upon.

However, what the masses tend to do is hardly ever the healthy or the right thing. If you look at the lives of the most successful people in the world, you'll realize that they greatly value solitude and quietness. I was reading a book by successful businessman and author John C. Maxwell. The book is titled *How Successful People Think*.

The entire book is dedicated to building the right kind of mindset and cultivating the type of thinking that is most conducive to success. Maxwell emphasizes the importance of spending time alone in peaceful solitude every day. According to him, this is absolutely critical for cultivating your ability to think independently and effectively (Maxwell, 2009).

If you want to be successful in life, then you have to dedicate some time every day to build a stronger relationship with yourself. Always remember that the most important relationship you are ever going to have is with yourself. Hence, this relationship must be prioritized above all else.

Besides, every other relationship you have in life is always going to be a magnified reflection of this one relationship. If you want to improve your relationships with others, then you have to first improve your relationship with yourself. You can never have a healthy relationship with another human being without first having a healthy and wholesome relationship with yourself.

DON'T RUN AWAY FROM YOUR THOUGHTS

Why do you think it is so tempting to spend hours in front of the television? Why is alcohol abuse so rampant in society? Why do we get sucked into the rabbit hole of social media when we go online to check our social media feed for just five minutes?

It is because all these things feel good in the moment. The problem is that they are mere distractions that give us an escape from facing uncomfortable thoughts, feelings, and emotions. They do nothing to help us address the real issue which is often emotional pain.

You can get a temporary escape by indulging in these activities but they also compel you to have a crash immediately after. After watching a movie marathon on Netflix, you feel guilty and disgusted with yourself. When the alcohol begins to wear out, it leaves you with gnawing despair and a pervasive sense of depression.

Also, just because you are consciously not thinking about something doesn't mean that the uncomfortable thoughts and emotions have disappeared. By suppressing thoughts and emotions, you can never get them to disappear. The harder you try to suppress them, the more forcefully they get pushed into the subconscious mind from where they continue to influence your behavior and mindset.

The only way to get rid of uncomfortable thoughts and emotions is by facing them. For this, you have to devote some time every day to spending time in quietude. Set some time aside every day to just sit with yourself. You don't want to resist any thought that comes up during this time. Instead, your goal should be to acknowledge and embrace them fully.

Something truly miraculous begins to happen once you start embracing all your thoughts instead of resisting them. These thoughts almost immediately stop bothering you – they arrive and dissolve in your consciousness like waves in the ocean. They stop pestering you because you are no longer trying to fight them.

Having the witness mindset is very important here. Instead of thinking you are the one who is having these thoughts, start looking at them from a distance from a third-person perspective. Observe how each thought arises in your consciousness of its own accord. Let it appear fully at the forefront of your mind – don't judge it or indulge it in any way. It will disappear quickly without bothering you much.

Unfortunately, we are taught to judge our thoughts. We are conditioned to believe that some thoughts should be encouraged while others have to be fought against. The problem with this ideology is that it goes against a fact of life: whatever we resist, persists.

It is also important to understand that each thought arises from a different part of you. You may think that the 'bad' thoughts you get come from the undesirable parts of you. The label you assign to it is a judgment towards that thought and the aspect of you from which it is arising.

In reality, you don't have any bad or undesirable parts. All parts of you function as a whole to make you the complex and magnificent human being you are. The "bad" "negative" and "pessimistic" thoughts you get arise from those parts of you that want to protect you.

For instance, if you have experienced heartbreak or disappointment in the past, then your mind may seek to caution you to not do anything that can lead to a reoccurrence of the same experience. It is your mind's way of protecting you, but if you judge those thoughts as "negative" and then seek to shun them from your consciousness, they'll start pestering you like the monster under your bed.

Dr. Richard Schwartz has written an excellent book on this subject called *No Bad Parts*. I would highly recommend that you read this book to understand how all the different aspects and parts of you are striving to do the very best for you. You really have no bad or undesirable parts (Schwartz, 2021).

Once you start understanding this idea, it becomes easier to not judge or resist those seemingly "negative" thoughts. Instead, you start listening to what your inner self is trying to tell you, and you become more compassionate towards yourself.

Allow yourself to feel all the emotions that arise in the landscape of your consciousness – each one has its own unique purpose. We cannot function as wholesome and complete human beings without allowing ourselves to experience the full spectrum of the human condition. It includes all thoughts and all emotions arising in our consciousness.

EXERCISE

Set aside 10 minutes every morning and evening to just be quiet and fully present with your thoughts and emotions. Remove all distractions – switch off your phone or put it on airplane mode. Tell your family you are doing something important, and they shouldn't come to you unless it was an absolute emergency.

If possible, try to maintain a dedicated room or a corner in your home where you can do this practice every day. You can also do it by going to a park and spending time alone in nature. Do what works best for you. Just make sure that there are minimal external distractions. Keep your environment as peaceful and quiet as possible.

When uncomfortable feelings, thoughts, and emotions start arising – do not resist them. Instead of judging them visualize them as waves arising and disappearing in the vast sea of your consciousness. Sit with the feeling of discomfort. After a while, it will stop bothering you. Practice being a witness – that's the most powerful technique you can master.

In the space below, write down when and where you'll be doing this practice every day.

PRACTICE JOURNALING

A lot of times, we don't realize or understand what our thoughts are until we begin to write them down. I would encourage you to maintain a separate diary or notebook dedicated solely to journaling. You can use a digital diary or notebook as well.

That being said, I feel writing things the old-fashioned way on pen and paper tends to be a lot more powerful when it comes to journaling. There is a lot of research that shows how writing with a pen and paper engages the brain in a more powerful way than typing (Jones, 2020). But if you absolutely don't want to use a physical journal, then using a digital one is okay. Anything is better than not doing it at all!

You can use journaling any time of the day to clarify your thoughts and ideas. Writing is an extremely powerful practice. It allows you to develop a deeper and clearer perspective on things. Journaling also enables you to feel lighter because when thoughts are confined to your mind, they often feel extremely overwhelming. By writing things down, you realize that it is usually just a handful of thoughts that your mind repeatedly brings up.

Journaling is an excellent tool for finding solutions. If you are confused about something, then writing down all your thoughts related to that subject will help you look at everything from a distance. You will be able to evaluate better what you should be doing to get the desired results.

I would strongly recommend that you do your journaling in a peaceful and quiet environment. Do your best to minimize distractions. This will help you dive deeper into your thoughts and emotions. You can practice journaling every day or whenever you are feeling overwhelmed by your thoughts. You can also do both – journal every day and also whenever you are feeling overwhelmed.

EXERCISE

Set aside a dedicated notebook or diary for journaling. Start using it immediately. You can write whatever comes to your mind in free flow or you can keep it centered around a specific topic where you would like to gain greater clarity.

I would also recommend that you regularly write down the answers to the questions I have shared below. These questions will help you develop immense self-awareness. Self-awareness is the master skill that you need in your arsenal for realizing all your big and small goals.

For now, you can practice by writing the answers to these questions here. Next time, you can copy these questions into your new journal and write the answers there. I would highly recommend doing this practice at least once a month. You'll be amazed by how your answers change as you grow and evolve into a better version of yourself.

Questions to Ask Yourself

What am I avoiding right now?

_____

_____

_____

_____

_____

What am I focusing on right now?

_____

_____

_____

_____

_____

What do I truly need to focus on **right now?**

_____

_____

_____

_____

_____

What is my highest priority right **now?**

_____

_____

_____

_____

What is my most important goal **right now?**

_____

_____

_____

_____

Am I doing things that take me closer to my goals, or am I spending too much time doing things that are taking me away from my goals?

What should I be doing more of?

What should I be doing less of, or should stop doing altogether?

_____

_____

DO SOMETHING CREATIVE

What do you enjoy doing the most? Is there something you have long wanted to do but can't seem to be able to prioritize it? Do you have a hobby that you genuinely love, but you no longer do it, or you don't give it enough time anymore?

It is important to be productive, but it is also crucial to schedule time regularly to nurture your hobbies and interests. Doing so will help you feel refreshed. You'll be able to get back to work with renewed energy. Creative activity performed for its own sake is also a wonderful tool for getting in touch with your core.

Some people think they are just not the creative type. I refuse to believe that. You only need to look at a joyfully playing child to realize that we are all born creative. At some point, you were also a small child – creative and enthusiastic. As you were growing up, maybe the adults around you told you to do more productive things. You heeded that advice, and slowly your creativity started slipping away.

I'm all for being focused and productive but creativity for creativity's sake has its own importance. Pursuing creative activities you enjoy allows you to just "be" and enjoy the moment. It replenishes your soul. Over time, this feeling of creative fulfillment seeps into all areas of life. Hence, you feel a lot more fulfilled with your life in general.

I would recommend that you get in touch with that inner child who was extremely creative at one point. That child is still alive inside you somewhere. Try to recall what it was that you enjoyed doing the most as a child. Maybe it was painting, making DIY crafts, or something else.

Try doing those activities now and also explore related hobbies. If you still can't figure out something you'd like to do, then research hobby classes. You'll get new ideas for what kind of hobby you can adopt. Try out different things, and then pick what you enjoy doing the most. Never feel guilty about investing time, energy, and resources into nurturing your hobby. It will pay off in more ways than you can imagine.

EXERCISE

Create a list of 10 hobbies that you may be interested in. Pick one from the list that you are feeling drawn to the most and start doing it.

_____

_____

_____

_____

I am ready to start pursuing

SET GOALS AND CREATE AN ACTION PLAN TO ACHIEVE THEM

Most people never achieve anything worthwhile in life primarily because they don't know what it is they want to achieve. To know your goals, you have to first know who you are. You have to identify your core values – the things that are most important to you. Real happiness can be experienced only when your core values and your goals are fully aligned.

To keep things simple, focus on just one goal at a time. Ask yourself what it is that you want to achieve this year. It should be something you truly want and are willing to pay the price for. You have to want something so bad that you are willing to do whatever it takes to get it. Again, knowing your core values and having a deep understanding of who you are as a human being is extremely important for setting appropriate goals.

If you aren't sure what your core values are, then it may take you some time to figure them out. Spend time analyzing what it is that you are really good at. Is there something you enjoy doing so much that you lose track of time while doing it? You can also ask your family and friends what they believe are your strengths. Think of those areas of life where others come to take advice from you. Having all this information will help you gain clarity about your core values.

When it comes to goal-setting, create a vision of what you would like your life to ideally look like a year from now, five years from now, and ten years from now. If that sounds like a lot to figure out, then start with just the one-year mark. What would you like to have achieved by the end of another year? Where would you be living? Who will be there in your life? How would you spend your days?

You must give yourself free rein to answer these questions. Right now, it may seem to you that what you want is impossible. Put your critical mind aside – just imagine what you would want if you knew that anything you wished for right now was going to come true. Put it in writing and trust that it is already yours.

Moving forward, research the people who have already achieved what you want to achieve. Try to learn as much about them as possible. What are their habits? How do they spend their time? What kind of people do they associate with? What is their body language like? How do they dress?

Researching the people who have the results that you want will give you the conviction that what you want is possible. If they can have it, then so can you! I can guarantee you that by learning more about them, you'll realize you have the same potential as them. You just need to start believing in yourself more.

You also need to start taking massive action to achieve your goals. Anyone who is sitting at the top didn't get there by a stroke of luck. Results require action. Outstanding results require massive action. Success is not something you stumble upon. It is something you create through hard work and persistent massive action.

Once you have defined and set your goals, I'd urge you to create an action list. It should include all the things you are going to do to achieve your goals. Create a sequence in which you will implement those action steps and then just get started!

Check in with yourself every day to see whether you are moving away from your goals or closer to them. Every single day of your life should be aligned with your goals. At the end of each day, take the time to define what you'd like to achieve the next day and also reflect on how much you have progressed that day. You don't have to spend a lot of time doing this. Even 5 minutes of self-evaluation is better than none.

On the weekend you can spend a little more time analyzing your progress and results. I would also advise you to create an action plan for the coming week. It doesn't have to be as detailed as your daily action list, but you do need to have an idea as to what you'd be doing in the coming week.

EXERCISE

Set some time aside to complete this exercise. Try to do this in a relaxed and calm state, away from all distractions.

Write down three core values that are most important to you.

_____

_____

_____

_____

What is your most important goal for the next year?

_____

_____

Write down at least five action steps you can take to achieve your goal. At least one of these action steps should be something that you can start doing immediately.

SCHEDULE THE TIME TO RELAX AND JUST BE

It is absolutely imperative that you regularly schedule the time to relax and just be. This should be the time that you spend doing nothing or you do only those activities that help you relax. You want this time to be as peaceful and nurturing as possible. For instance, you can spend time in nature or you can create a peaceful environment at home by lighting some candles and playing soft music.

The goal here is to slow down and become fully present in the moment. You can also schedule a massage to help yourself relax deeply. Do whatever feels good to you! Give yourself the freedom to simply enjoy this time by yourself away from all responsibilities, demands, and obligations.

I would strongly recommend that you schedule at least one hour every week to relax deeply. If you feel this is impossible for you, then I would urge you to reassess your life, and how you are allocating your time. Maybe you are trying too hard to do everything on your own. Practicing radical self-love means staying open to receiving help from others. For this, you have to be willing to ask for help – give others the chance to do something for you. Your loved ones really do want to support you – you just need to tell them exactly how they can do it.

A lot of people struggle with delegation because they believe they are the only ones who can perform a task satisfactorily. Nothing good can come out of being such a perfectionist about everything. If someone else can perform a task at least 80% up to the standard you have set for it, then it is worth delegating that task.

You can also hire paid help wherever necessary to reduce your burden. Don't put so much strain on yourself. Do the best you can, but prioritize your well-being above all else.

EXERCISE

Schedule one hour this week to relax and just be. Specify which day and at what time you are going to do it. Be sure to follow through on your commitment.

_____

_____

_____

_____

_____

_____

5

HAVE A VISION FOR YOUR LIFE AND FOR WHO YOU WANT TO BE

"A vision is not just a picture of what could be; it is an appeal to our better selves, a call to become something more."

— ROSABETH MOSS KANTER

In our modern society, almost everyone boasts of being busy. But how many people have a vision for their life and for who they want to be? Some will even say they are too busy to create a vision for themselves. How counterintuitive does that sound? Busyness without a vision is akin to running around in circles like a hamster on a wheel. To get to your destination, you must first sit down and determine exactly where you want to go.

Think about it – do you just get inside your car and start driving without a destination in mind? Obviously not! That would be crazy. Why would you waste your time, energy, and money driving aimlessly? Yet when it comes to their own life most people keep driving helter-skelter without any idea of where they want to go or how they are going to get there.

I think the biggest reason why most people don't have a vision for their life or for who they want to be is because they believe what they want will never happen. As children, we used to genuinely believe anything and everything was possible. Growing up, the adults around us started telling us how this or that wasn't possible.

We were told to dream within our limits and not to spread our wings too far wide lest we may fall. What they accepted as their own truth, they attempted to transmit to you. Their ideas and beliefs about life are not facts but are projections of their own limited worldview onto you.

Now, maybe you are wondering why talk about things like goals and vision in a book about radical self-love. I want to discuss these topics with you because authentic self-love is not about taking a break from your regular life to sometimes do things that nurture your body, mind, and soul. It is about creating a life that you love so much that you do not need to take a break from it at all.

To truly fall in love with yourself and your life, you must develop intense self-awareness. You can't accept yourself completely unless you acknowledge and understand who you are. Similarly, you can't love your life in the truest sense of the word without practicing gratitude for all the blessings you already have while doing the work to get what you want.

Even if you don't believe what you want is possible, isn't it better to die trying to create what you want than to live a life of hopelessness? Besides, when you have a burning desire for something and you are willing to move beyond all your self-imposed limitations to achieve your goals, all the forces of the Universe align to support you.

You are the only person who knows what your dream is and you are the only person who can turn your dream into a reality. You have to first start believing that what you want is possible. If there is just one person in this world who has what you want, then that means it is possible for you as well. Never envy anyone. Instead, look at others for inspiration.

Celebrate all successes – including those of others. Something miraculous begins to happen when you get in the habit of celebrating both your own successes and those of others.

The Universe starts recognizing that you are someone who really likes success. So you start receiving more reasons to revel and celebrate.

THE DIFFERENCE BETWEEN A GOAL AND A VISION

Since we discussed goal setting extensively in the previous chapter, I think it is important to create a clear distinction between a goal and a vision. On one level, it may seem like they are the same, but that's not true.

A goal is a milestone of achievement that you set for yourself within a specific timeline. For instance, it may be something you want to achieve a year down the line, two years down the line, and so on. Vision, on the other hand, is something that encompasses your entire life. It is the larger picture within which everything occurs. Vision is like the vast infinite sky while big and small goals are like planets and stars in that sky.

Your vision encompasses the larger picture of what you want your life to be like while your goals are smaller pillars of achievement that contribute towards materializing it. If you haven't thought about your vision yet, then it is time you do it now. A life without a clear vision is in many ways a life without meaning.

You can set accurate goals for yourself only when you know what your vision for yourself and your life is. Otherwise, you may achieve what you set out to achieve only to realize that it isn't really what you wanted in the first place. If you completed the exercises in the previous chapter, then by now, you would have a clearer idea about your core values. Knowing your core values is essential for crafting an inspiring vision for your life. So if you haven't completed the exercises in the previous chapter, then go back right now and complete them.

YOUR VISION SHOULD BE YOUR OWN

From childhood, we are told who we should want to be – study hard, get a decent job, get married, and have children. Even if you manage to hit all these goalposts, you may still feel deeply unfulfilled. This generic template of what success should be like doesn't make most people happy.

You may or may not want all the items on this list. The biggest thing that is missing from the list is the acknowledgment of your own individual mission, purpose, and vision. We are not taught to think of life in these terms, but that's what is essential for experiencing authentic fulfillment.

We live in a society where consensus and conformity is rewarded from an early age. We are taught to regurgitate premade answers instead of being encouraged to think for ourselves. As adults, we have to do a lot of unlearning if we want to be genuinely happy.

Each one of us is unique and irreplaceable in our own way. You have come into this world to do something that is completely unique to you. You have to identify what YOUR vision for your life is. I am not talking about the vision that family, friends, and society have given you, but the vision you carry deep inside your own heart.

It is time to step into the light and fully own this vision. This is where your power and your potential lie. All dreams can be realized. You don't have to know how your vision will turn into a reality, you just have to fully embrace it. The Universe will pave the way for it to be realized. Of course, you need to do your part as well by taking massive action daily – do the work and leave the rest to the Universe. Life will continue to unfold in magical ways and your vision will continue turning into a reality.

You must take your chances and **allow** yourself to believe in all possibilities. Whatever you **want** is within your reach. You just have to be willing to **shed** the baggage of your limiting beliefs and reach for the sky – quite literally!

EXERCISE

Take the first steps towards creating a vision for who you want to be and the type of life you want to live by answering these questions.

What is it that moves you? (Your vision should fill you with positive emotions and enthusiasm.)

_____

_____

_____

_____

What do you long for?

_____

_____

_____

_____

If you knew that whatever you wanted was going to happen, what would you ask for?

_____

_____

_____

_____

What kind of a person do you have to be to live this dream life?

_____

_____

_____

_____

IDENTIFYING YOUR MISSION AND PURPOSE

Your mission and your purpose are other important pieces of the puzzle that are essential for creating your ideal vision. Your mission summarizes what you are here to do. Your purpose gives you the motivation and the drive to pursue that mission.

For instance, let us say you are a counselor. Your mission can be "to help people explore and embrace their fullest potential." Your purpose can be "to make the world a better place by helping others realize their fullest potential in this life."

Your vision for your life is "to spend every day of life doing something good for others." Your vision for yourself is "to be the kind of person who adds tremendous value to other people's lives."

I hope, by now, it is becoming clear to you what the difference between your mission, purpose, and vision is. Even if it is still not clear to you, there is no need to fuss too much about it. Just write what makes sense to you right now. You can always refine and modify things later on. In fact, as you keep learning, growing, and evolving into a higher version of yourself, you'll feel compelled to redefine all aspects of your life.

It is also possible that you have already evolved to a level where you have great self-awareness about who you are and what you want out of life. In that case, your vision, purpose, and mission statements may remain the same for the rest of your life. Just keep in mind that nothing is set in stone. You can always revisit these things and redefine them to suit who you are at the time or who you want to be.

Most people never give any thought to these things. You are already much further ahead in the game by simply attempting to define your mission, purpose, and vision. You don't have to get everything right immediately, but you definitely need to take the first step right away. The longer you'll put off defining your mission, purpose, and vision, the greater you'll delay living the life of your dreams. Don't be just another one of the masses who are trapped in the limited paradigm that was given to them by others. Let your magnificence shine – your time is NOW!

EXERCISE

Write down your mission, purpose, and vision statements as succinctly as possible. Let it be short and precise – one or two lines at the most. These statements should evoke a strong emotional response in you. Every time you read them, you should feel excited and enthusiastic. If they don't affect you at a deep emotional level, then keep refining them until they do.

It's okay if you can't get to that point right away – write everything down anyway. If you keep working on your statements, eventually you'll reach a point where they begin to feel powerful and inspiring. Simply getting started and consistently taking action are the only real keys to success.

My mission in life is

My purpose in life is

My vision for my life is

My vision for myself is

TURN YOUR VISION INTO A REALITY

Knowing your vision is essential but taking action to turn that vision into a reality is even more important. In the absence of massive action, goals, and vision become mere wishful thinking. Nothing worthwhile can be achieved in life without consistent massive action. I have said this before, and I'll say it again: taking action isn't enough – you need to take massive action! Taking massive action once in a while is also not enough – you have to consistently take massive action.

What does it mean to take massive action? It means you challenge yourself to get more done than most people do in a week, a month, or a year. We try to convince ourselves that we are doing our best but taking a closer look often reveals that we are operating at or below 40% of our intrinsic capacity. Next time, you think you are doing your best or that you have given your all, ask yourself if it is really the truth.

I am absolutely sure your answer will be "No," provided you are being completely honest with yourself. You have infinite potential for growth and excellence. You can always do better than what was your best yesterday. Growth is the one and only constant in the experience of human life. What is not growing and evolving is decaying and dying. If you want to thrive in life, then you have to constantly challenge yourself to do better today than how you were doing things yesterday.

When you are beginning to feel tired or you think you have done enough, challenge yourself to stretch yourself by another 10% to see what you are capable of. Once you achieve that, challenge yourself to stretch by another 10%.

Keep doing it constantly and consistently – you'll be amazed by how much potential you have for growth and excellence.

I am not suggesting that you should push yourself so much that you get burned out. On that note, I feel it is important to define this word properly. This term gets tossed around a lot and almost everyone thinks they are experiencing burnout when in reality they are not even operating at their optimum capacity. I experience burnout only when my heart, mind, and soul are not aligned with what I am trying to accomplish. So if you think you are going through burnout, it is time to really evaluate who you are and what you want out of life.

The distance between your dreams and reality is called action

If you study the lives of the most successful people in the world, you'll realize they all have one thing in common – they love their work! It is extremely difficult to work hard at something you hate doing. You can do it for some time, but encountering burnout is inevitable in that case. Successful people work all the time, but they don't get burned out because they love their work.

I understand that you may not currently be in a position where you can claim to love your work – that's alright! It took me a very long time to figure out who I am and what my purpose in life is. Besides, it's not enough to adopt a profession you love. You also need to make sure that there is a market for it. You need to be able to make money while enjoying working on your passion. So there has to be a demand and a marketplace for what you want to offer.

When you love your work, you'll be more committed to polishing your skills and abilities. Hence, you'll be able to stand out more in your field or niche. The more distinct and irreplaceable you become, the higher you are going to rise in your career.

In other words, taking massive action in a field of work you actually enjoy is much easier than struggling to take massive action doing something you hate. If you haven't figured out what you love doing, then keep exploring. Continue diving deeper into your core values. The better you understand your mission, vision, and purpose, the easier it will be for you to identify a career that suits you.

Having a career doesn't always have to mean working at an office. Maybe your core value is investing in your family. In

THE RADICAL SELF-LOVE WORKBOOK FOR ADULTS | 113

that case, your vision can be about living a fulfilling family life. You may want to materialize that vision by being a housewife or househusband. That is also totally fine! You have every right to live life on your own terms. There is no one size fits all solution for everyone.

You must do what is best for you even if no one else agrees with you and you to go against the grain. Think about it – a hundred years from now you and everyone else whose opinion you care about won't even be around in this world. Is it really worth giving up on your dreams and your vision to please someone else?

Each one of us has come into this world with a very unique purpose. We must embrace and honor it wholeheartedly. Never hold yourself back from living your best life just because you fear other people's opinions and judgment.

Authentic radical self-love is all about valuing your own opinions and priorities above what others want of you. Besides, every human being is flawed. If others have an opinion about how you should be living your life, it is essentially only a projection of their own biases and limitations.

While you are likely going to have only one mission and one primary purpose in life, you do need to have different visions for each area of your life. You can have one all-encompassing vision for your life and then also have a separate vision for each area of your life. You can set goals for each area of life according to the vision you have for it.

Just make sure that your goals and vision for all areas of life are in alignment with your mission and purpose. In other words, your vision for each area of life should not contradict your mission and purpose. To live a fulfilling life, your purpose and mission need to be fully aligned with the vision you have for the different areas of life.

If you are brand new to all this, then I'll suggest you go slow, taking just one step at a time. Trust me, taking one small step at a time is better than attempting giant leaps in one go. The latter will likely cause you to fall flat, but the former will ensure that you keep making consistent progress toward your goals.

If developing a vision for all areas of your life and having goals associated with each area sounds extremely over-whelming, you can pick just one area that is most important to you right now. It should be an area that you know would have the highest impact on improving the quality of your life. Start working on this area immediately.

As you make progress in this one area, you can start evaluating other areas of your life as well. Over time, you'll be in a better position to develop a vision for and set goals in other areas of your life as well. Success begets greater success. Once you start seeing results in one area of life, you'll automatically feel more motivated to work on improving the other areas of your life.

EXERCISE

Out of the following key areas of life, pick one that is most important to you right now. It should be an area where you know any improvement will have the highest positive impact on the quality of your life right now.

Circle the area of life that you want to work on right now:

Health and Fitness

Career

Finances

Relationships

Intellect

Environment

Spirituality

Charity and Giving

The most important area of life for me right now is _____. For now, I am whole-heartedly going to focus on mastering _____.

Write down your vision for this most important area of life. Make sure that this vision is fully aligned with your mission and life purpose.

Write down all the roadblocks you are going to face as you work on turning this vision into a reality.

Write down the potential solutions for these roadblocks. No matter how insurmountable a problem may seem, there is always a solution for everything. If you can't find the answer right now, then give it time – sit with the problem a little longer. Research how other people have overcome the same issues. Seek out people who have the results you want to create and learn from them.

To be successful, you have to develop a solutions-oriented mindset. Instead of allowing yourself to get emotionally bogged down by problems, you have to put aside all your emotions and focus on logically finding answers and solutions. Emotions enrich our experience of life by allowing us to feel and experience life deeply, but they can also become a roadblock to our success when we give them free rein. You should witness all your emotions like waves arising and dissolving on the ocean floor, but don't let them control you.

From now on, I want you to operate with the mindset that there is a solution for everything. Once you start believing this truth, you'll be amazed by how solutions begin to (almost miraculously) appear. Once you get yourself out of your own way, you can start seeing the possibilities and solutions that have always been around. Yes, they are there even right now! All you have to do is remove the blindfold of your limiting beliefs to see them clearly.

Write down all the steps you are going to take to turn your vision into a reality. Break things down into smaller milestones or goals. Be sure to assign a timeline for achieving each milestone. Ask yourself what you need to achieve next week, next year, in 5 years, in 10 years, and so on.

Focus your energy on what you can achieve immediately within the next week and a month. If you keep moving forward one step at a time, you'll keep getting closer to your dream life. For now, your ultimate goal may seem impossible or improbable, but if you'll consistently keep taking action, then you'll definitely achieve it.

Create your plan right now and start taking action on it from today. When I say today, I mean TODAY! Even if it is a very small step, you've got to start today. That is how you communicate with the Universe. It is a way of saying, you are truly ready to receive what you are asking for, and you are committed to doing whatever it takes to fulfill your desire.

_____

_____

_____

_____

_____

_____

_____

_____

_____

_____

_____

_____

_____

_____

_____

State your commitment to turning your dreams into a reality
– you are going to persist no matter what.

I   commit   to

6

CONFRONT YOURSELF AND MASTER YOUR EMOTIONS

"Our deepest fear is not that we are inadequate. Our deepest fear is that we are powerful beyond measure. It is our light, not our darkness that most frightens us."

— MARIANNE WILLIAMSON

I f you have completed all the exercises in the previous chapter, then you are likely feeling all fired up. You are ready to start, but there is a voice inside your heart whispering to you all the reasons why you won't succeed. As the euphoria of motivation begins to wear off, this voice becomes louder and more overpowering. You start believing all the nasty things it says: "You can't do this" "Who do you think you are?" "You have nothing of value to offer to the world." The list goes on and on.

Whether you are willing to believe this or not, the truth is you are 100% responsible for the life you are living right now. You are the sum total of the choices you have made so far. If you are wondering why you would create all the undesirable things in your life, then let me tell you why. You have created them in ignorance. No one taught you that every choice you make influences the outcome of your life. A series of bad choices leads to what the average person describes as "bad luck."

Practicing radical self-love is all about assuming radical responsibility for your life. I am not saying that you have to blame yourself for every single negative thing that has happened to you. All I am saying is the moment you point the finger at someone or something else, you make yourself powerless. You become a victim of circumstances, and when you are a victim there isn't much you can do to change the situation. You are at the mercy of others. Is that how you want to live your life?

The only person standing between you and your dream life is YOU! We are often our own worst enemies. We set new goals enthusiastically, and then sabotage our chances of success. If you want to live an extraordinary life, then you have to stop thinking like an ordinary person. Most people live a life of passivity.

They never take responsibility for their life or for who they are. Turning your dreams into a reality begins by stepping into your full power. That can happen only when you start taking radical responsibility for your life. Don't make yourself powerless by believing in the narrative of "poor me." You are an infinitely powerful being – you have the power to turn all your dreams into reality.

FACE YOUR FEARS

The things we are afraid of the most are the things we need to do the most. It is within these challenges that the seeds of massive growth are hidden. You'll never realize what you are truly capable of if you keep pushing all your demons under the rug. They don't go away like that. To make them go away, you have to confront them.

Fear is a primal emotion. Most of the time, fear has nothing to do with the thing or circumstance you are associating it with. Think about all the people in this world who are able to do the thing that scares you so much. If your fear was logical or factual, then everyone in this world would have the same experience with it, but that's not the case.

The worst thing about fear is that it paralyzes your ability to think or act. Your throat becomes dry, your heart starts pounding, and your palms become sweaty. Worst of all, your mind becomes foggy.

It is important to understand that even the most courageous person in the world has fears. Fear is part and parcel of the human experience. The highly courageous person has just learned to deal with it better. The more often you look fear in the eye and overcome it, the more courageous you become. Being courageous is a choice, and so is staying fear-ful. You have to choose who you want to be. Your fear has nothing to do with actual facts or circumstances. It has everything to do with YOU. You have to face your own self to overcome that monster you fear so much.

It is not an exaggeration to say that everything worthwhile you want is on the other side of fear. Most people don't succeed because they want rewards without making sacrifices. You have to make sacrifices by doing the things you fear or hate doing. There is no way around it. You can either live a life of mediocrity or you can unleash your greatness. To do the latter, you have to go where most people aren't willing to go – inside that deep dark cavern where your deepest fears reside.

Fear can never be overcome by trying to ignore or forget about the things you fear. To overcome fear, you have to look it in the eye and overcome it by applying grit and determination. Also, most people think that they will be able to do what needs to be done only after their fears have completely disappeared. That is again faulty thinking. You have to persist in your efforts by doing what is needed despite the fear.

Fear should never be resisted because you give greater power to it by resisting it. Instead, you have to overcome fear by embracing it fully. Allow yourself to feel the fear, but do what you need to do in spite of what you are feeling.

THE IMPORTANCE OF EMOTIONAL CONTROL

Fear is an emotional reaction to real or imagined threats. It is a crippling emotion. Fear reduces your power to take action if you allow it to control you. The same goes for all emotions. Emotions deepen our experience of life when we are in control of them. But they can cripple and disempower us if we allow our emotions to control us.

Easier said than done – I know! It does take practice to start being in control of your emotions. The good news is that the more frequently you practice, the better you get at it. No one is born with these character traits. Well, some people are indeed a lot more emotionally sensitive than others. To be successful in life, you have to master the skill of handling emotions effectively.

Our success in all spheres of life depends upon our ability to control our emotions. Developing emotional control is essential for steering the wheels of destiny in your favor. Without emotional control, you cannot make good decisions. The foundation of success is built by consistently taking good decisions.

Think about it – The affection and joy you feel when something wonderful happens makes life beautiful. Life will be so bland if you couldn't feel all these beautiful emotions. On the other hand, think about what happens when you are deeply fearful and anxious about something.

If you are like most people, then you'll label the first example as something positive, and the second one as negative. I used to do that as well. On some level, it isn't wrong. However, in reality, things are a lot more nuanced. There are really no undesirable emotions – all emotions are to be felt and experienced in their fullness.

I know this is contrary to what most modern-day coaches will tell you. You are constantly told to think positive and stay away from "negative" thoughts. It's like asking someone to not think of a pink elephant. The moment you tell someone not to think about it, all they can see inside their mind's eye is a pink elephant. Also, this idea that certain parts of us are undesirable or certain emotions are to be refrained from is a flawed concept.

Everything in nature has its own purpose and significance. We wouldn't have been endowed with these universal human emotions if they didn't have a purpose. Besides, it isn't just you but every single human being on the planet who experiences this full spectrum of human emotions.

You don't need to resist emotions like anger, disgust, fear, or sadness. You need to embrace them. By embracing them, you'll allow yourself to see what your core is trying to tell you through these emotions. For instance, the part that is fearful of making that dreaded phone call may be trying to protect you from the pain of rejection that you felt the last time you did something similar. Once you start realizing that these emotions and those parts of you from whom they stem aren't your enemies but your allies, everything changes.

Instead of putting all your energy into resisting them, you can listen to them. It is amazing how these monsters that we fear so much dwindle and diminish once we stop putting so much energy into resisting them. Embracing all aspects of yourself is the only effective strategy for creating your dream life.

THE EMOTIONAL MASTERY QUIZ

This quiz will help you understand whether you are in control of your emotions or they are in control of you. It will help you understand how much work you need to do. Again, this is not about beating yourself up for your shortcomings. Use the results of this quiz as a tool of empowerment. No matter where you are in life, you have the power to change your destiny.

Creating the life of your dreams and becoming the person you want to be is entirely in your own hands. It doesn't matter what your results turn out to be – the only thing that matters is what you do with them. I always say this and I am going to repeat this one more time: transformation begins with self-awareness and a firm decision to change. Who you have been so far doesn't have to determine who you are going to be from this day onward. You are the only one who has complete power over you – exercise it constructively to become who you have always wanted to be.

I would recommend that you take this quiz after every few months, or maybe annually, to see how much you are in charge of your emotions. Sometimes we are doing a lot worse than we think we are, and at other times, we are actually doing better than we realize. Quizzes like these are excellent for developing greater self-awareness and for acquiring an objective view of how things are.

For each question, give yourself a score on a scale of 0-4. This is what each number indicates: 0 = strongly disagree, 1 = disagree, 2 = neutral, 3 = agree, 4 = strongly agree. Use the scoring guide at the end of this quiz to understand your results.

1. At least 90% of the time, you feel calm and collected.
2. You don't take important decisions when emotions are high. Like, when you are extremely happy and excited or extremely sad and dejected.
3. You think rationally even under pressure.
4. You have mastered the art of thriving on challenges.
5. You don't fear change.
6. You are extremely resilient.
7. You feel negative emotions, but they don't bog you down for too long (not any more than a few hours).
8. You generally don't do or say anything in a state of anger that you'll regret later.

9. You can't remember the last time you had an emotional outburst.
10. When things get challenging, you're the one who tells others to stay calm.
11. When challenges come up, you immediately start thinking about solutions.
12. You firmly believe that there is a solution to every problem. You are fully committed to finding the solution every time you encounter a problem.
13. Others think of you as a positive and uplifting person to be around.
14. You are extremely optimistic.
15. You keep your eyes fixed on the light at the end of the tunnel no matter how dark things are looking.
16. You genuinely believe every challenge is an opportunity to grow and become better.
17. You believe you have the power to weather any storm and emerge victorious on the other end.
18. You don't get too excited about your wins even though you know how to celebrate them.
19. Disappointments and setbacks can never hold you down for too long.
20. After each setback, you come back stronger and more determined to win.
21. You believe you are 100% responsible for your life and everything in it.
22. You believe your happiness is your responsibility alone.

23. You know and fully understand that happiness is a skill that can be learned.
24. You are always in a good mood.
25. You laugh and smile very frequently.
26. You know how to fill each day with joy and beauty.
27. You go to bed with gratitude in your heart.
28. You are grateful to be living your best life right now.
29. You know how to truly enjoy the company of your loved ones.
30. Your loved ones like having you around.

Your Total Score: _____

SCORING GUIDE

Use this guide to understand your results.

100-120 – You have really mastered your emotions. You are doing very well. Emotional mastery is the key to success in all areas of life. Make a note of all those statements where your scores were lower. These are areas where you can grow more. Personal development is a never-ending process. You can always grow more and become more.

The human potential for growth is infinite. This is a wonderful thing – the more you become, the more you can have and enjoy life! Never put a cap on what's possible – stay committed to your personal development and keep growing.

70-100 – You have mastered your emotions to a large extent. This is great! Now, it is time to identify what your major weaknesses are. Check your scores to find out your weaknesses. The statements where you scored the lowest will show you the areas where you need to focus on improving. Don't let this information bog you down. Instead, use it as a tool of empowerment.

Most people don't dare to take an honest look at themselves. You are already doing something that the masses never do. By knowing your weaknesses, you can work on them until they become your strengths. Keep in mind that happiness and emotional control are learnable skills. You have the power to master your emotions and live a life of great happiness.

>70 – You struggle with your emotions. They often get the better of you. The good news is you do have the ability to control your emotions. It is a skill that anyone can learn. It doesn't matter what your starting point is, you can reach your destination if you are committed to it. Identify the statements where you scored the lowest. These are your blind spots. Knowing, admitting, and embracing your weaknesses is the most important step in the journey of transformation.

In the rest of this chapter, I am going to share with you practical tools, tips, ideas, and methods that will help you with emotional mastery. Be sure to read everything attentively and do all the exercises. Always remember that happiness and emotional control are skills that can be learned. You can master your emotions if you are fully committed to making it happen.

THE ART AND SCIENCE OF MASTERING YOUR EMOTIONS

The quality of your life is determined by the quality of your emotions. Hence, emotional mastery is absolutely essential for creating and living a fulfilling life.

I want to share with you practical tools, tips, methods, and strategies that you can immediately start practicing. Understanding things theoretically is not enough for gaining mastery over your emotions. You get results only by practicing what I am sharing with you in this chapter. The more frequently you practice, the better you'll get at it.

Deep Breathing

What happens when you are in a state of fear or anxiety? Your breathing becomes shallow and your throat begins to feel dry. The best and the most effective way to deal with a panic attack is by gently pulling your mind away from the thoughts that are causing you anxiety or fear and focusing your attention entirely on your breath. Simply close your eyes and start observing the inflow and outflow of each breath.

Observe how each breath is flowing inside your nose – visualize and feel it spreading inside your body. As the breath is spreading inside your body, feel each cell of your body getting illuminated with positivity, hope, and joy. As you breathe out, visualize all the fear and negativity getting expelled in the form of a ball of black energy leaving your body.

If it is difficult for you to do this visualization, then you can also just count 1-8 for each breath that is going in and 1-8 for each breath that is going out. So with each inhalation, you'll count 1-2-3-4-5-6-7-8. With each exhalation, you'll count 1-2-3-4-5-6-7-8. Breathe deeply from your stomach and not just from your chest. With each inhalation, your chest and stomach should expand fully. With each exhalation, your chest and stomach should contract completely.

You can also combine the counting exercise with the visualization practice to enhance your focus further. If you feel comfortable doing just the visualization or just the counting exercise, then that is also good.

Exercise

Take a few minutes to practice deep breathing in the manner I have explained above. Moving forward, devote at least five minutes every morning and evening to practice deep breathing. If you start doing this right after waking up and immediately before going to bed, you'll benefit tremendously.

I would also encourage you to get in the habit of practicing it whenever possible. I mean in addition to your morning and evening practice. Yes, you can also do it with your eyes open when it is not possible for you to close your eyes. Closing the eyes helps in focusing better. But when doing so is not an option just do the best you can with your eyes open.

It is especially useful whenever you are feeling anxious, fearful, or perplexed. Just bring your mind into the present moment and focus on your breath. You'll immediately start feeling calm, centered, and more grounded.

Create a statement of commitment to incorporate this practice into your daily routine.

I commit to

_____

Reframing

This is my favorite strategy for dealing with challenging life situations. No two people have the exact same reaction to the same situation. This is because no two people have the exact same mental framework for assessing and understanding a situation.

Our mental frameworks are built through the life experiences we have had and from the conditioning we receive growing up. Most people don't realize that their reaction to a situation isn't the only way one can respond to it. If you want, you can completely reframe things, thereby, transforming your perception of the situation and your reaction to it.

Let me explain this more clearly with an example. Two twin brothers grew up in an extremely abusive household. One becomes a massively successful businessman who contributes to and establishes charities that protect abused children. The other brother becomes an alcoholic who eventually dies from a drug overdose.

Both brothers grew up in the exact same circumstances and faced the exact same challenges, yet they went on to live completely different lives as adults. What is the reason for this?

This is because the successful brother used the challenges to fuel his desire for a better life. The drug-addict brother perceived himself as a victim of circumstances. Hence, he never made the effort to turn the wheels of destiny in his favor.

You can either allow your challenges to bog you down or you can use them to fuel your dreams and passions. You can either be a victim of your circumstances or you can be the one who uses every obstacle to evolve into a higher version of yourself.

The moment you start blaming anyone or anything outside of yourself, you give your power away. It is better to focus on how you can turn your adversities into abundance. You have the power to do it. Once you reframe your perception of the challenging situation, you can identify the blessing that is hidden inside it. Nothing negative can ever happen to you when you are determined to turn every challenging situation into something positive and favorable.

The thing that helps me the most is to always remember that I am here to learn and grow. No matter what situation comes up in life, I can always learn, grow, and become better. By adopting such a mindset, you can make the best of whatever cards you get dealt.

Exercise

Write down a negative situation that bothers you a lot.

_____

_____

_____

Now, think of the blessing that can come out of this situation. Identify how you can learn from this situation and grow into a finer version of yourself. Write everything down in the space below.

Moving forward, what actions are you going to take to turn the challenging situation into a blessing? Write down at least five action items in the space below with at least one being something you are going to do immediately within the next seven days.

7

MAKE THE TIME TO NURTURE YOURSELF DAILY

"With every act of self-care your authentic self gets stronger, and the critical, fearful mind gets weaker. Every act of self-care is a powerful declaration: I am on my side, I am on my side, each day I am more and more on my own side."

— SUSAN WEISS BERRY

I was about to title this chapter "take the time to nurture yourself daily" and then it occurred to me that "take" sounds like you are taking something away from your schedule. Self-care is a gift that you give to yourself. Hence, the word "make" fits in better here – you DESERVE to "make" the time for yourself every single day. You are worthy and deserving of your own love.

I know it is hard for a lot of people. Society constantly bombards us with the idea that making time for ourselves is selfish. We start feeling like any time we are making for ourselves is time that we are taking away from our family and loved ones. Nothing can be farther from the truth.

Taking excellent care of one's own self is not only the most important act of unconditional love, but it is also a moral responsibility. When you don't make the time to look after your own needs, you start expecting others to fill your empty cup. As I said earlier, no one can ever give you what you don't have for yourself.

Ignoring your own needs doesn't serve anyone. If you are constantly prioritizing other people's needs at the expense of your own, it will eventually make you resentful. No one understands you and your needs better than you. You have to do what is necessary for you whether anyone else agrees with it or not. That being said, I have always found that loved ones tend to be very supportive if we explain properly why we need some separate "me-time." If you are surrounded by people who don't want to understand this need of yours or they simply refuse to be supportive, then it may be important to take a deeper look at those relationships.

Either way, you can never please everyone in this world. No one can ever fulfill your needs completely unless you learn to give yourself the fulfillment you are seeking. Other people can add to your joy, happiness, and bliss. If you are waiting for them to fill your pitcher in its entirety, then you must realize that it is just too much to ask for from any human being. You are setting yourself up for disappointment.

HOW TO MAKE TIME FOR YOURSELF NO MATTER HOW BUSY YOU ARE

If you are one of those people who is so busy that you have no time to look after yourself, it is high time you take a step back and start evaluating how your constant busyness is impacting you and your life. We live in a society where being busy or at least claiming to be busy is often seen as a badge of honor. Ask any person if they have time for this or that, and they'll retaliate by saying how busy they are.

Take care of yourself

There is a difference between being busy and being productive. You could be slaving away for 15 hours a day, but if you are not performing at an optimum level, your results won't be commensurate with the toil you are going through.

You don't need to work more hours to be productive. You can get more done in a shorter amount of time if you are mentally, emotionally, and physically performing at your peak level. It is very hard to be productive when one is constantly feeling tired or burnt out. Self-care is not a waste of time or for that matter a luxury. It is an absolute necessity! You won't expect your phone to serve you without charging it every day. Why would you expect your body, mind, and emotions to serve you if you are not doing anything to intentionally replenish your energy levels every day?

Self-care is the most productive thing you can do as it enables you to be more effective and efficient throughout the day. If you want to be highly energetic and extremely productive, then you must take excellent care of yourself. You don't have to take my word for it. For the next 21 days, just follow everything I am sharing in this chapter. If it doesn't change your life for the better, then you can come back to me and tell me how wrong I am. But I can promise you that won't happen!

When your cup is full, you show up stronger and more effective in all areas of life. Self-care leads to self-improvement, and relentless self-improvement is the master key for realizing all your life goals. Keep in mind that you can never experience authentic self-love without intense self-care. Your most important responsibility is to look after yourself.

You are the only one who stays with you eternally. Hence, the relationship you have with yourself is always going to be the most important relationship you can invest in. The more you invest in your relationship with yourself, the stronger you become. Self-care is an excellent investment of your time and energy into YOU.

On that note, let us discuss some practical ways in which you can schedule time for daily self-care in your routine.

Allocate Some Time Where You Belong Only to You

If you have never before prioritized your needs, then chances are you may not get the most enthusiastic response from your near and dear ones if you suddenly tell them you need some time by yourself. It is normal for humans to resist change. When we make dramatic changes to our lives and self, it can make the people around us uncomfortable. They may become fearful of losing their relationship with you, but if they truly love you, they'll eventually understand.

People are also often a lot more supportive if you get them involved in some way. For instance, you can ask them for help with performing some of your responsibilities. Explain to them just how much you'll appreciate their help if they can take care of some things for you so you can use that time to recharge yourself. Never say something like you need a break from your relationship as that can make others feel threatened which would give rise to conflict.

Instead, focus on telling them how their support of your self-care routine enriches your life. Focus on explaining to them how taking care of your own needs will help you be a more pleasant and enjoyable person to be around. If they accept the offer of helping you, be sure to appreciate their efforts by complimenting them generously. Never take anyone for granted. By showing your gratitude and appreciation, you increase the chances of winning over their constant support.

If you live by yourself and you are responsible only for your-self, then you won't have to face this challenge. Either way, make sure that you are spending some time completely cut off from the world.

Use this time to connect with yourself by doing something that replenishes and recharges you. For instance, you can spend time meditating, reading inspiring books, working out, etc. Try to switch off your phone, computer, television, and all other sources of information in your environment. It will help you listen to the voice of your own soul loud and clear.

Exercise

Write down all the self-care practices that you enjoy doing. These should be things that help you feel refreshed, rejuvenated, and replenished.

_____

_____

_____

What can you do to reduce your stress levels? Who can you ask for help?

_____

_____

_____

Wake Up a Little Earlier

I am not suggesting that you should wake up at 4 or 5 am every day. You just need to wake up early enough to spend some time charging your batteries for the day ahead. You don't want to get out of bed and start your day in a reactive mode. Taking the time to prepare for the day will help you feel you are in charge. If you wake up late and start the day in reactive mode, it feels as if everything is spiraling out of control.

You want to have at least half an hour where you can just be by yourself and do what is important to you in that time. If you can schedule an hour or more, then that's even better! Waking up just half an hour earlier than usual to practice some self-care is guaranteed to dramatically change your life.

To wake up early, you have to go to bed early. Instead of making a drastic change to your schedule, start by going to bed just one minute earlier than usual and wake up just one minute earlier than usual. Over the next 60 days, increase this time by one minute every day. By the end of the 60-day period, you will be waking up half an hour earlier. It is easier to implement small incremental changes that compound over time to create dramatic results.

When implementing new changes, always remember the good old proverb that slow and steady wins the race.

Exercise

How much time would you like to devote every morning to your self-care routine?

_____

_____

_____

Do you need to wake up earlier to have some undisturbed "me time" every day? What should be your wake-up time? What changes are you going to make to your schedule to accommodate your new self-care practices?

_____

_____

_____

_____

_____

_____

_____

_____

_____

. . .

Take Small Breaks Throughout the Day

Taking short breaks throughout the day to indulge in some self-care will definitely improve your productivity. It doesn't matter whether your work involves being an executive, a CEO, or a housewife, you do need to take regular breaks. Breaks are essential for refreshing your mind and recharging your batteries.

By being more intentional with your time, you can use your breaks to replenish your energy. The keyword here is "intentional." The time you spend mindlessly scrolling social media won't help you feel recharged and replenished. On the contrary, it will drain you and leave you feeling depleted. I am sure you already know the feeling I am talking about.

Personally, I like to use the Pomodoro Technique to maximize my productivity throughout the day. It is a time management method developed by a man called Francesco Cirillo (Cirillo Company, n.d.). The technique involves working in spurts of 25 minutes followed by a five-minute break. In the 25-minute period, you cut out all distractions and focus only on the job at hand. It is easier for the mind to concentrate intensely when the goal is to do it only for 25 minutes. When the mind knows that you are going to get a five-minute break at the end of the 25-minute period, it cooperates better.

Each 25-minute spurt is known as a pomodoro. At the end of four pomodoros, you can take a longer break of 20-30 minutes. During the breaks, it is best to do something that gets you to move your body. For instance, you can take a walk or maybe even do some light stretching. Also, use the breaks to drink some water and grab a healthy snack if you need one.

The Pomodoro Technique can be used for performing all kinds of tasks. Whether you are mowing the lawn or writing a business report, you can use it to be more productive and efficient. It is especially helpful when working on difficult tasks that seem overwhelming. There are many websites and apps that can help you with tracking your pomodoros. Just find one you like and start timing yourself. You can also do it the old-fashioned way by using an alarm clock and manually tracking your progress on paper. Do what works best for you.

The only thing I would caution you against doing is mindlessly scrolling your phone during breaks. I am not saying that you can never do that, but we all know how one minute of "just checking updates" turns into an hour or two of mindlessly browsing online. If you want, you can set aside some time every day where you get to freely browse the web. It must be done once all the important tasks for the day have been. Always be intentional with your time.

I would also recommend that you impose a time cap on how long you are allowed to mindlessly browse the internet every day. For instance, you can give yourself 30 minutes every day where you can do things like watch TV or mindlessly browse news feeds. At the end of the 30 minutes, your alarm will go off, and you'll leave whatever you were doing.

Using this strategy will help you stay in charge of your time. You won't feel guilty because you'd know you have earned that time to do as you please. That being said, be very careful to not let yourself fall into the trap of "just one more minute" when the alarm goes off. One minute easily becomes five, 20, 30 minutes, and so on.

The feeling of not being in control of your actions induces a gnawing sense of guilt. To experience self-love, you have to practice self-discipline. You have to get into the habit of doing what is best for you instead of caving into the temptation of doing whatever you feel like in the moment.

Exercise

Which self-care practices would you like to do during your short breaks?

_____

_____

_____

_____

_____

_____

Important Self-Care Practices that You Should Implement in Your Life

In this section, I am going to share with you some of the most important self-care practices that are essential for leading a happy and fulfilling life. You don't have to implement all of them immediately. In fact, I would advise you against it as you'll likely end up feeling overwhelmed. Smaller changes made gradually over a longer period often create better transformations than drastic changes made in a short time.

I would suggest that you identify just one thing that is most out of balance for you right now and focus on fixing that. Pick something that is going to have a very high impact on all areas of your life. For instance, getting enough sleep is the most important self-care practice because if you are not getting proper rest, you won't be able to function at peak energy levels.

Lack of sleep also takes a massive toll on the body and mind. It can even offset the benefits of healthy eating and regular exercise. Getting proper sleep will hugely impact all other areas of your life as you'll have more energy for doing everything better. This is just one example. Maybe your situation is different. Like, if you are suffering from lethargy, then working out every day may get you the highest return on investment.

In short, pick one thing that would impact your life the most and stick with it for at least a month. In fact, I would say 90 days. In my experience, it takes much longer than 21 or 30 days to really form a habit. At the end of the 90-day period, you can pick something else that you want to focus exclusively on. The interesting thing is if you make one positive change, then it will automatically have a domino effect on all the other areas of your life.

For instance, going to the gym daily will motivate you to eat healthier. You'll find yourself making better food choices simply because you don't want to sabotage your progress in the gym. This is a wonderful thing. You really don't have to force yourself to adopt all the healthy self-care practices at once. Just focus on one thing at a time. As you make progress, maintain the habit you have already built and then keep adding new ones on top of it.

Proper Sleep

For a very long time, I treated sleep in the same way as most youngsters do. Yes, I thought it was something optional. It's only much later in life that I began realizing the toll that chronic sleep deprivation takes on the mind and body. Now, I am not suggesting that every single person should sleep a specific number of hours every night. In my opinion, that kind of advice is good as saying everyone in the world needs to eat the exact same diet.

The truth is people have different physiological and psychological makeup. The amount of sleep you need may be completely different from what I need. You are the only one who knows what the optimum amount of sleep for you is. I would strongly recommend maintaining a sleep journal where you note down the amount of sleep you are getting each night along with a short note about how you were feeling when you woke up.

I would also recommend noting down the time when you are falling asleep and the time when you are waking up. In my experience, when we are going to bed and when we are waking up are far more important factors in determining the quality of rest we receive than merely counting hours.

If I sleep at 3 am and wake up at 11 am, I feel extremely lethargic and tired even though technically I have had 8 hours of sleep. On the other hand, I wake up refreshed and energetic when I go to bed at 10 pm and wake up at 4 am. Technically, it is less sleep but, in my experience, the hours don't matter nearly as much as when we are going to bed and when we are waking up.

Ideally, our sleep schedule should be in sync with nature's rhythm of day and night. To learn more, you can read about the body clock system that Chinese medicine talks about. Ayurveda also discusses this subject in depth. If you research "dinacharya," you'll find out what Ayurveda recommends for a healthy daily routine. I would advise you to educate yourself in this area and then craft out a sleep schedule that works best for you.

Exercise

How would you rate your sleep quality on a scale of 1-10, with 1 being very low and 10 being exceptionally good?

What would your ideal sleep schedule look like – at what time do you see yourself going to bed every night and waking up each morning?

Start maintaining a sleep journal where you record when you went to bed, when you woke up, and how many hours of sleep you got. Also, take notes about the quality of sleep you are having.

Healthy Diet

I don't believe in there being just one ideal diet that everyone in the world should stick to. Your ideal healthy diet depends a lot upon your health status, fitness goals, lifestyle, and other unique factors.

In general, I can tell you that it is best to cut out all food items that have colors, additives, and other chemicals. Try to stay away from ready-to-eat food items as much as possible. Instead, focus on eating fresh fruits, vegetables, and whole grains.

You are the best person to know what kind of diet works for you. If you really aren't sure how to create a good diet plan for yourself, then you can consult a professional fitness trainer or a qualified dietician to help create your custom diet plan.

Again, my recommendation here is that you be a lot more intentional with your choices. Opt for natural and unprocessed food items as much as possible. Stay away from chemical-laden items.

Exercise

What does your ideal diet plan look like? Take help from a professional if you aren't sure about how to create a custom plan for yourself.

Start maintaining a food journal where you are writing down everything you are eating in a day. The simple act of recording your food choices will make you a lot more conscious of what you are putting in your mouth. Don't put off doing this until a time in the future when you are hoping to get your diet on track. You need to start this process right now!

Regular Exercise

Moving your body regularly is absolutely essential for maintaining good health. The human body is not designed to remain in a sedentary position all day every day. I am not suggesting that you must get a gym membership if that's not something you want to do. I would say it is far more important to get in the habit of making healthier choices throughout the day than devoting an hour in the gym. The latter is important, but what you are doing the rest of the 23 hours is even more important.

Being a healthy and fit person requires thinking differently. You have to train yourself to make better choices throughout the day. For instance, take the stairs at work instead of the elevator. Consider walking to places instead of driving everywhere. Being healthy and fit is a lifestyle and not just an activity confined to a specific hour of the day.

On weekends and holidays, you can invite all your loved ones to do some activity together. Like, you can all ride a bike or go hiking. You can also play sports together. Like, volleyball, basketball, etc. Think creatively and plan activities that you know everyone will enjoy and that everyone you are inviting has the physical capacity to participate in.

Exercise

Write down at least five things you can implement in your daily life that will help you move your body more. For example, going to the gym, taking the stairs, playing volleyball on the weekends, etc.

Slowly start adding these activities to your daily routine.

Regular Relaxation and Meditation

I would highly recommend that you regularly take the time to relax your body, mind, and spirit. It can be anything from weekly massages to daily five-minute meditation.

I would strongly suggest that you add meditation to your daily routine. You can find a simple guided meditation online that you truly resonate with and start using it every day. You can also try out different types of meditation depending on how you are feeling each day.

Meditation helps make you really present in the moment and that is the key to authentic happiness and radical self-love.

By being fully present in the moment, you can easily love and accept yourself on all levels.

A lot of people claim that they just cannot meditate. If that sounds like you, then you are likely wondering how you can meditate when your mind jumps around too much to let you sit still. Believe it or not, that's everyone's mind.

Yes, even the most seasoned meditation practitioners have a monkey mind. They have just trained themselves to deal with it better. If you stop fighting your mind's tendency to jump from one thought or idea to another, and, instead, accept whatever comes up, it will stop troubling you so much.

You always want to think of thoughts as waves arising on the ocean floor. Let them arise and subside on their own. You'll be amazed by how quickly the negative thoughts disappear once you stop fighting against them.

Just try out meditating for the next 14 days. You'll be amazed by the benefits – I promise!

Exercise

What are the activities that you can implement in your daily life to relax your body, mind, and spirit? Write down at least five suggestions.

Once you have your list ready, start implementing each suggestion one at a time.

8

PRACTICING THE ART OF HAPPINESS

"Happiness is a choice you make and a skill you develop. The mind is just as malleable as the body."

— NAVAL RAVIKANT

Staying happy and joyful is not something that just happens to you without you putting in any effort. It is a skill that you develop through deliberate practice. But first, you have to consciously decide to be happy. Yes, being happy is a matter of choice and decision.

Most people think that happiness is something that just happens on its own. Nothing can be farther from the truth. You can put 10 people in the same situation and each one will respond to it differently. Some people will find what is wonderful about the situation and will choose to be happy. Others will find something negative even in the most favorable set of circumstances.

In short, people who have developed the skill of happiness will figure out how to find joy and happiness in all situations. On the other hand, those who have developed the habit of constantly complaining will find a reason to complain about things no matter how well everything is going.

Happiness is, therefore, a matter of perspective. If you want to be happier, then you must commit to cultivating happiness. Slowly, your perspective will start shifting, and you'll become the type of person who sees the good in every situation.

HAPPINESS BEGINS WITH ACCEPTANCE

The feeling of unhappiness arises only when we allow ourselves to think that something is missing from life. This is why a person can be extremely happy living in a mud hut with a leaking ceiling and another person can be miserable even while living inside a grand luxurious palace. Happiness has very little to do with our outer circumstances – it is dependent largely upon our internal state.

If you'd allow yourself to believe that something is missing from your life, then you'll automatically feel unhappy. Instead, if you can get yourself to accept life just the way it is, then you can be fully present in the here and now. The present moment is where happiness is experienced in its full glory.

Now, I am not suggesting that you should become smug and not aspire for more in your life. Absolutely not! I am all for constant growth and improvement. The idea here is to aspire for more while being grateful for what you already have.

Whoever you are, whatever you are experiencing, and everything you have right now is the sum total of all your past decisions. Since the past is history, there is nothing you can do about it. Your power lies in the here and now. You can change the future you are creating for yourself by making better choices today.

The same idea applies to self-acceptance. You accept who you are today with unconditional love and gratitude while constantly aspiring to be better. You don't have to be disdainful towards yourself or your life in order to be a better person and experience a better life.

Gratitude is undoubtedly the perfect antidote to sadness and negativity. By being grateful for all the blessings you have in your life, you can immediately shift your perspective. Even if you think there is nothing to be grateful for in your life right now that can never be true. If you have food on the table, a roof over your head, and this book in your hand – you already have a lot to be grateful for.

The problem with us humans is that we often don't value what we have until we no longer have it. If you feel there is nothing in your life to be grateful for, then that means you are taking a lot of things for granted. If you start counting all the big and small things that are going well in your life right now, then you'll definitely come up with a long list of things to be grateful for.

Exercise

Create a list of at least 10 things that you are grateful for in your life right now. Be sure to include both big and small things.

_____

_____

_____

_____

_____

_____

_____

_____

_____

_____

_____

Write down at least 10 things you have in your life right now that, in the past, were things you wished for. It can be something small like a favorite outfit you were finally able to buy or something big like the career of your dreams. I am sure if you think hard enough, you'll easily come up with at least 10 things that were once a dream but are now part of your reality.

From now on, every morning write down at least three things you are grateful for. Challenge yourself to come up with something new and different every day. Be sure to include both big and small things in your list. Even having a pen to write with or a computer to type on are things to be grateful for!

By starting your day with gratitude, you'll train yourself to retain a more positive attitude throughout the day.

I'll also suggest that whenever you are feeling low or negative, you create a list of at least 10 things you are grateful for. Gratitude truly is the most powerful practice for immediately shifting your mood and mindset. Think of it like this – when you are feeling negative or depressed, your head is turned in the wrong direction. Gratitude immediately turns your head in the right direction helping you focus on all your blessings and all the positivity that surrounds you.

THE IMPORTANCE OF ENERGY MANAGEMENT

Time management is a hot topic. Everyone wants to know how they can manage their time better. There are countless tools and methods that promise to make one more efficient and effective. The problem is time management tools rarely ever work. At least, they never worked for me!

I would create a really demanding timetable for myself, and then I'll fail to stick to it. It is akin to trying to go on a diet. Very soon, you begin feeling like a total failure as forcing yourself to stick to anything brings up a lot of resistance and negativity in your psyche.

Eventually, I came upon this idea of energy management. People always say time is money. Time is regarded as the most valuable resource in the world. My perspective is slightly different. I feel there is only so much energy we have throughout the day and how we allocate tasks depending upon our varying energy levels determines how much fulfillment we'd get out of our day. Efficient energy management is absolutely essential for being happy.

For me, this implies holding a clear distinction in my mind as to which activities deplete my energy reserves and which ones energize me. For instance, working on a business report often leaves me slightly depleted. I have to balance it by engaging in an activity that replenishes my energy reserves. For instance, meditation energizes me. So after working on a business report for 4 hours, I may take a half an hour break to meditate.

I must clarify here that just because an activity requires a depletion or expenditure of energy doesn't mean that it is something bad or negative. Energy is the currency with which we experience life. In the simple process of living life, we do have to expend the energy that we are constantly generating and accumulating. The key to living a fulfilling and happy life lies in realizing which tasks require a higher expenditure of energy and then intentionally balancing them by also engaging in activities that energize you.

It is like driving a car. In the process of driving, you are going to use up fuel – that's not a bad thing. It is simply a necessity and a natural consequence of living life. Just like how you constantly keep refueling the gas tank at regular intervals, you have to do the same thing to the same for building your energy reserves.

For instance, an hour-long run may leave you feeling depleted even though it is excellent for your health and fitness. You can recharge yourself by playing with your children for half an hour (if it is something that helps you feel energized).

This strategy is also excellent for building good habits. Reward is a better teacher than punishment. By constantly rewarding yourself for all the positive actions you are taking, you can program yourself to do more of those good things.

Exercise

Create a list of all the activities that you perform on a typical day. Classify them as "ED" (energy depleting) or "ER" (energy replenishing). Pair each ED activity with an ER activity. This way, you will keep refueling your tank throughout the day.

_____

_____

_____

_____

ASSESS YOUR PRIORITIES

Most people live their life on auto-pilot. They do the same thing day in and day out without thinking much about what they are doing. Mastering the skill of happiness requires intentional living. It is easy to take life for granted when you are feeling you'd be here forever, but we all know human life is defined by its brevity.

In the grand scheme of things, if you just sit down to calculate the length and span of the average human life, you'll realize that none of us have that much time here. I am not saying this to invoke fear in you. I personally feel it is very liberating to realize that none of us are going to be here forever.

If you are afraid of doing certain things because of what other people would think, then I would urge you to look at it from a different perspective. Think about it – 60 or 80 years from now it is likely that none of those people whose opinion you fear so much would be around. Maybe by then, you won't be around as well. When you are on your deathbed would it really seem worthwhile that you gave up your dream because of the opinion of others?

Once you start taking decisions keeping in mind the brevity of human life, it becomes easier to do the things you are afraid of doing. There is only so much time you have here. It is better to live this life in accordance with your core values instead of striving to constantly please others at the expense of your own goals and dreams.

Happiness is something you experience when you are living a life that is true to your core values. Again, knowing your core values is very important for living a fulfilling life. You also need to have a vision for what you want your life to be like and for who you want to be. Of course, nothing is set in stone.

As you keep growing, your goals, dreams, and vision will also likely evolve and change. But at any given point in time, you do need to know who you want to be and how you want to live your life.

Exercise

What are the things you want to do that you are not doing right now because of fear or uncertainty? Create a list, then pick one thing that is most important to you right now, and just do it! If you can't do it right now, then give yourself a deadline (a specific date and time) by which you MUST do it.

EXPECT LESS FROM OTHERS AND MORE FROM YOURSELF

Expecting too much from others is the number one happiness killer. A person who expects too much from others just cannot be happy. No matter how close someone is to you, they are an individual in their own right. You can't control their behavior and actions. Your expectations not only sabotage your peace of mind, but they also negatively impact your relationship with the other person.

When you are doing something for others, it should be from your heart. Never do anything expecting something in return. The act should be its own reward. This way, you aren't dependent on someone else's actions to give you what you need. You already have the peace and contentment you need. Any acknowledgment or gift the other person gives you becomes a bonus. Hence, you are better able to appreciate what they are giving you.

Being happy means being self-reliant. You have to train yourself to depend upon yourself to meet all your needs. Of course, you should ask others for help whenever you need it. You can tell them exactly what they can do for you, but beyond that don't harness any expectations. Whether the person chooses to meet your needs or not is entirely upon them. You have to do what's best for you and sometimes this means walking away from a relationship where your needs are not being met.

By practicing self-care rituals and doing things that meet your needs, you keep your own cup full. Other people can add to that happiness, but you aren't dependent on anyone to get your needs met.

Exercise

What are your expectations from others that are currently not being met?

_____

_____

_____

_____

How can you fulfill those needs on your own?

Are your communicating your needs clearly in your relationships? What action do you need to take in the relationships where your needs are currently not being met?

HELP OTHERS

Ultimately, life is measured by the impact we have on others. Helping others unconditionally is one of the most rewarding things in life. When you do something for someone else without any hidden agenda, it does something to you at a very deep level. You are able to double up your fulfillment because you get to feel the fulfillment of the other person along with your own.

"You have not lived a perfect day unless you've done something for someone who will never be able to repay you."

— RUTH SMELTZER

As human beings, we are social creatures. We thrive in communities. We need each other to function effectively as a society. At the spiritual level as well, we are all connected. When we do something good for another soul, we are also doing good for ourselves. Besides, the Universe rewards every positive act. Whatever we give comes back to us multiplied

That being said, you should never do something for someone if you are looking for rewards or even acknowledgment. Do it because it feels right and because it is what you genuinely want to do. Only then, it is guaranteed that your good deeds will be rewarded. When you are not attached to the outcome, it doesn't really matter whether you receive something back or not. But you will!

This attitude is the master key to living a blessed and happy life. By doing good, you attract good things into your life. When you are not expecting anything and you receive a reward for your good deeds, it makes you very happy. This is so much better than expecting too much and feeling disappointed because you didn't receive what you wanted.

You don't always have to do big things to create a huge impact on someone's life. Sometimes a small act of kindness like a heartfelt smile or an uplifting compliment can make someone's day.

Give happiness to others and you will automatically become a happier person. Do things for others without expecting anything in return. Perform acts of kindness out of the goodness of your own heart. You'll be amazed by how incredible it feels to put a smile on someone else's face. Don't let this be an isolated act you do once in a while. Develop the habit of helping others unconditionally on a regular basis.

Exercise

Think of one person whom you can help right now. Write down exactly how you can help them. Once you have the answer, just take action on it!

A SHORT MESSAGE FROM THE AUTHOR

Hey, are you enjoying the book? I'd love to hear your thoughts!

Many readers do not know how hard reviews are to come by, and how much they help an author.

Customer Reviews

★★★★★ 2
5.0 out of 5 stars ▾

5 star		100%
4 star		0%
3 star		0%
2 star		0%
1 star		0%

See all verified purchase reviews ›

Share your thoughts with other customers

Write a customer review

I would be incredibly grateful if you could take just 60 seconds to write a brief review on Amazon, even if it's just a few sentences!

Thank you for taking the time to share your thoughts!

Your review will genuinely make a difference for me and help gain exposure for my work.

S. S. Leigh

CONCLUSION

I hope you have enjoyed this journey toward greater self-love. If you completed all the exercises, then I am sure you have undergone a shift in how you feel about yourself and your life. If you haven't completed all the exercises, then I would urge you to go back and complete them.

Reading a book is powerful, but to change your life you have to take action. By reading a book, you can feed your mind new ideas, but unless you put things to practice the information you are absorbing won't benefit you much.

Also, don't let this be one of those books that you read once, and then it just gathers dust on your bookshelf. Keep coming back to this workbook. Maintain a journal where you can practice the exercises again after a few weeks or months.

Compare them to everything you had written in this workbook. I am sure you'll be amazed by the progress you make. Keep repeating this process every couple of months.

Every time you come back to this workbook, you'll develop new insights and perspectives. You'll learn more about yourself and about your life. The content of the book remains the same but it is you who will evolve more by the next time you come back to this book. As you grow, your capacity to understand and perceive things at a different level also transforms. You start observing things that weren't obvious to you before.

As human beings, we have infinite potential for love and growth. The more you grow as a human being, the greater self-love you'll experience. All relationships require time and effort. This is just as true for your relationship with yourself as it is true for your relationships with others. You have to nurture your own self if you want to have a deeply fulfilling relationship with yourself. No relationship is as rewarding as a lifetime of romance with one's own self. Whatever investment you are making in this one relationship right now is guaranteed to be totally worthwhile in long run!

I would urge you to continue the practices that you have adopted through this workbook. If you want to add something extra, then I would suggest checking out my "I Am Capable Project - Daily Affirmations" book series. In those books, you'll find unique affirmations that you can add to your morning, afternoon, and evening routines respectively.

Be sure to invest in yourself every single day. Nothing is more powerful than falling in love with yourself over and over again.

Sincerely,

S. S. Leigh

REFERENCES

Banks, T. (n.d.). *Tyra Banks quotes*. BrainyQuote. Retrieved October 23, 2022, from https://www.brainyquote.com/quotes/tyra_banks_452188

Berry, S. W. (n.d.). *A quote by Susan Weiss Berry*. Goodreads. Retrieved October 23, 2022, from https://www.goodreads.com/quotes/10377421

Brown, B. (n.d.). **Quoted in** *50 self-love quotes to boost your confidence and Lift your spirits*. Good Housekeeping. Retrieved October 23, 2022, from https://www.goodhousekeeping.com/life/g38333580/self-love-quotes/

Jones, A. M. (2020, October 4). *New Study suggests handwriting engages the brain more than typing*. CTVNews. Retrieved October 23, 2022, from https://www.ctvnews.ca/health/

new-study-suggests-handwriting-engages-the-brain-more-than-typing-1.5132542

Kanter, R. M. (n.d.). *Rosabeth Moss Kanter quotes*. Brainy-Quote. Retrieved October 23, 2022, from https://www.brainyquote.com/quotes/rosabeth_moss_kanter_390507

Maxwell, J. C. (2009). *How Successful People Think: Change Your Thinking, Change Your Life*. Center Street.

Owen, S. (n.d.). *A quote from Resilient Me*. Goodreads. Retrieved October 23, 2022, from https://www.goodreads.com/quotes/9064580

Pareto principle. Wikipedia. (n.d.). Retrieved October 23, 2022, from https://en.wikipedia.org/wiki/Pareto_principle

The Pomodoro® Technique. Cirillo Company. (n.d.). Retrieved October 23, 2022, from https://francescocirillo.com/products/the-pomodoro-technique

Ravikant, N. (n.d.). **Quoted in** *Happiness is a choice*. Almanack of Naval Ravikant. Retrieved October 23, 2022, from https://www.navalmanack.com/almanack-of-naval-ravikant/happiness-is-a-choice

Schwartz, R. (2021). *No Bad Parts: Healing Trauma and Restoring Wholeness with the Internal Family Systems Model*. Sounds True.

Smeltzer, R. (n.d.). *A quote by Ruth Smeltzer*. Goodreads. Retrieved October 23, 2022, from https://www.goodreads.

com/quotes/120222-you-have-not-lived-a-perfect-day-unless-you-ve-done

Williamson, M. (n.d.). Goodreads. Retrieved October 23, 2022, from https://www.goodreads.com/quotes/928

Winfrey, O. (n.d.). *A quote by Oprah Winfrey*. Goodreads. Retrieved October 23, 2022, from https://www.goodreads.com/quotes/2587-when-you-undervalue-what-you-do-the-world-will-undervalue

Made in United States
Troutdale, OR
11/11/2023

14492066R00106